XSLT 1.0
Pocket Reference

Evan Lenz

Beijing · Cambridge · Farnham · Köln · Paris · Sebastopol · Taipei · Tokyo

XSLT 1.0 Pocket Reference
by Evan Lenz

Published by O'Reilly Media, Inc., 1005 Gravenstein Highway North,
Sebastopol, CA 95472.

O'Reilly books may be purchased for educational, business, or sales
promotional use. Online editions are also available for most titles
(*safari.oreilly.com*). For more information, contact our corporate/
institutional sales department: (800) 998-9938 or *corporate@oreilly.com*.

Editor:	Simon St.Laurent
Production Editor:	Marlowe Shaeffer
Cover Designer:	Emma Colby
Interior Designer:	David Futato

Printing History:

August 2005:   First Edition.

0-596-10008-6
[C]

Contents

CHAPTER 1

Data Model

XSLT is a language for transforming XML documents. The input to an XSLT program (a "stylesheet") is one or more XML documents. The output is another document, which may be XML, HTML, or text. XSLT operates on an abstraction of XML, called the XSLT data model (the XPath data model with some additions). XSLT is "closed" over this data model. In other words, its data model applies both to its input and its output. In fact, it even models the stylesheet, which is itself expressed in XML.

TIP

Unless explicitly followed by "2.0," whenever this book speaks of "XSLT" or "XPath," it is referring to the 1.0 versions of these languages.

Node Types

The XPath data model describes an XML document as a tree of nodes. There are seven types of nodes:

root	text
element	attribute
processing instruction	namespace
comment	

In the XPath 1.0 data model, all XML documents have a single *root node*, which is an invisible container for the entire document. The root node is not an element.

TIP

XPath 2.0 uses the term "document node" instead of "root node." Regardless of what it's called, don't confuse it with the "root element" or "document element," which is an *element*: a child of the root node, or document node.

There is one *element node* for each element, one *attribute node* for each attribute (excluding namespace declarations), one *comment node* for each comment, and one *processing instruction node* for each processing instruction (PI) that occurs in an XML document. A contiguous sequence of character data, after expanding all entities and CDATA sections, is modeled as a single *text node*. Finally, there is a *namespace node* attached to each element for each namespace/prefix binding that is in scope on that element. Each element has its own unique set of namespace nodes, which always includes at least one namespace node that corresponds to the implicit mapping between the prefix "xml" and the URI "http://www.w3.org/XML/1998/namespace" (reserved for attributes such as xml:lang and xml:space).

TIP

Thus, even for a document that does not explicitly use namespaces, there will be as many namespace nodes as there are elements.

Node Properties

Table 1 lists four node properties and their applicability for each type of node. These properties deal with a node's relationship to other nodes. If a table cell is grayed out, that means the property is not applicable for that node type.

Table 1. Node relationship properties

Node type	Parent	Children	Attributes	Namespace nodes
Root		Ordered list of 0 or more elements, PIs, comments, and text nodes		
Element	Element or root	"	Unordered list of 0 or more attribute nodes	Unordered list of 1 or more namespace nodes
PI	"			
Comment	"			
Text	"			
Attribute	Element			
Namespace	"			

In the XPath language, to access a node's parent, child nodes, attributes, or namespace nodes, use the corresponding axis: parent, child, attribute, or namespace. See the section "Axes" in Chapter 2.

TIP

Attributes and namespace nodes are not children. An element is considered to be the parent of an attribute or namespace node, but the attribute or namespace node is not considered to be the element's child.

The *descendants* of a node consist of the node's children, its children's children, and so on.

All nodes, regardless of their type, have a *string-value* and a *base URI*. Some types of nodes have an *expanded-name*, which consists of two strings: a local part and a namespace URI. Element nodes have an optional *unique ID*. For each of the string-typed node properties, Table 2 lists the node types it applies to and how its value is determined. Once again, if a table cell is grayed out, that means the property is not applicable for that node type.

Table 2. String-typed node properties

Node type	String-value	Expanded-name (local/URI)	Base URI	Unique ID	Unparsed entity URIs
Root	Concatenation of descendant text nodes' string-values, in document order		URI of the document entity		A set of mappings between declared entity names and their URIs
Element	"	**Local:** local name **URI:** namespace name	URI of external entity; otherwise, base URI of root	Value of attribute declared as type ID in DTD (optional)	
PI	Text following PI target and whitespace	**Local:** PI target **URI:** null	"		
Comment	Content of comment		Base URI of parent node		
Text	Character data (at least one character)		"		
Attribute	Normalized attribute value	**Local:** local name **URI:** namespace name	"		
Namespace	Namespace URI	**Local:** namespace prefix **URI:** null	"		

The XPath language provides functions for directly accessing most of these properties. To access the string-value of a node, use the string( ) function.

To access the local and namespace URI parts of a node's expanded-name, use the local-name( ) and namespace-uri( ) functions, respectively.

The base URI property is used for resolving relative URIs in a document, and it is used by XSLT's document( ) function and the xsl:import and xsl:include elements. XSLT/XPath 1.0 does not provide a direct way to access the base URI property.

The unique ID property is queried by the id( ) function to retrieve elements according to their ID value. There is no function to access the unique ID property directly, but that is not normally necessary, since you can easily access an element's attribute values using the attribute axis.

Finally, use the unparsed-entity-uri( ) function to retrieve the URI of an unparsed entity with a given name.

All of XPath and XSLT's built-in functions are described in Chapter 5.

CHAPTER 2

The XPath Language

XPath 1.0 is the expression language embedded in XSLT 1.0. This chapter lists the primitives of XPath, including its four data types and how expressions of each type are evaluated.

Data Types

An XPath expression returns a value that has one of the following four data types:

- Node-set (an unordered collection of zero or more nodes without duplicates)
- Number (a floating-point number)
- String (a sequence of Unicode characters)
- Boolean (true or false)

Result Tree Fragments

XSLT adds one more data type to this list, the *result tree fragment*, which is created when an xsl:variable or xsl:param instruction uses content rather than the select attribute to define a variable. For example, given the following instruction, the value of $var will be a result tree fragment:

```
<xsl:variable name="var">
  <foo>text</foo>
  <bar/>
</xsl:variable>
```

A result tree fragment behaves like a node-set that contains one root node, except that certain operations allowed on node-sets are forbidden on result tree fragments. Result tree fragments can be converted to strings and copied to the result tree like regular node-sets, but the /, //, and [] operators are disallowed. Thus, the expression `$var/foo` is illegal. The only way to select the above `foo` element in XSLT 1.0 is to use an extension function that first converts the result tree fragment to a node-set, as in `exsl:node-set($var)/foo`. See Chapter 6.

TIP

XSLT 2.0 removes this restriction, abolishing the data type "result tree fragment" altogether. In XSLT 2.0, you can create "temporary trees" that are normal node-sets, so that, given the above example, the expression `$var/foo` by itself is legal and requires no extension functions.

Expression Context

All XPath expressions are evaluated in a context. The context consists of everything not present in the expression itself that may affect the resulting value of the expression. It consists of six parts:

- The *context node*
- The *context size*, an integer 1 or above (returned by the `last( )` function)
- The *context position*, an integer 1 or above (returned by the `position( )` function)
- A set of namespace/prefix declarations in scope for the expression
- A set of variable bindings
- A function library

XSLT specifies how the XPath context is initialized. See the "Processing Model" section in Chapter 3.

The namespace/prefix bindings and variable bindings are determined respectively by the namespace declarations and xsl:variable or xsl:param instructions in the XSLT stylesheet that are in scope for the attribute that contains the XPath expression. The function library consists of all of XPath and XSLT's built-in functions, as well as any extension functions supported by the XSLT processor.

The context of a sub-expression may differ from the context of the whole expression. In particular, the expression context changes inside predicates. See the upcoming section "How Location Paths Are Evaluated."

Kinds of Expressions

Table 3 shows an exhaustive list of the kinds of expressions in XPath 1.0. All XPath expressions fall into one of these eight categories.

Table 3. Examples of different XPath expressions

Expression category	Data type returned	Examples
Variable reference	Any	$foo, $bar, etc.
Function call	Any	starts-with($str, "a") true( ) round($num)
Parenthesized expression	Any	(//para) (foo | bar) (2+4)
Literal	String	"foo", 'bar', etc.
Number	Number	13, 24.7, .007, etc.
Node-set expression	Node-set	/html/body/p[2]/text( ) //@person | //person (.//note | para/fnote)[1] $ns[@id='xyz']

Table 3. Examples of different XPath expressions (continued)

Expression category	Data type returned	Examples
Arithmetic expression	Number	`(($x - 5) * 2) div -3` `$pos mod 2`

Boolean expression	Boolean	`$is-good and $is-valid`
		`$x >= 4`
		`position( )!=last( )`

Variable references start with a dollar sign ($) and refer to variables or parameters in the XPath expression context. Function calls are explained in Chapter 5 in the "Function Reference" section. Parentheses can be placed around any expression in order to control operator precedence. The remaining kinds of XPath expressions are covered next under the node-set, string, number, and boolean categories.

Node-Set Expressions

Node-set expressions include:

- Location paths
- Union expressions—union of two node-set expressions using the union (|) operator
- Filtered expressions—a predicate applied to any expression using the predicate operator ([...])
- Path expressions (any expression composed with a location path using the / or // operators)

The location path is the most important kind of expression in XPath.

Location Paths

A *location path* is an expression that selects nodes relative to the context node. There are two kinds of location paths: relative and absolute.

A relative location path consists of one or more *steps* separated by /. An absolute location path consists of /, followed by an optional relative location path. A / by itself selects the root node of the document that contains the context node.

TIP

This is usually the root node of the source tree, but it may be a different root node—for example, when using the document( ) function to select secondary input documents.

An absolute location path (other than / by itself) is evaluated by evaluating the relative location path that follows the /, using the root node as the context node.

Steps

A *step* consists of three parts: an *axis*, a *node test*, and zero or more *predicates* (see Figure 1).

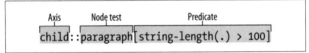

Figure 1. Syntax of a step

The axis specifier in the previous example is child::, the node test is paragraph, and the predicate is [string-length(.) > 100]. From left to right, here is how a step is evaluated:

1. The axis identifies a set of nodes relative to the context node.
2. The node test acts as a filter on that set.
3. Each of any number of optional predicates in turn acts as a filter on the set identified by the preceding predicates and node test to its left.

Axes

The *axis* of a step determines in what "direction" nodes are selected, starting at the context node. It identifies a set of possible nodes to select in relation to the context node. There are 13 XPath axes. Table 4 lists what each axis contains, relative to the context node.

Table 4. What each XPath axis contains

Axis	What it contains
child	The children of the context node.
descendant	The descendants of the context node; i.e., children, children's children, etc.
parent	The parent of the context node, if there is one.
ancestor	The ancestors of the context node; i.e., parent, parent's parent, etc.
following-sibling	All nodes with the same parent as the context node that come after the context node in document order (empty if the context node is an attribute or namespace node).
preceding-sibling	All nodes with the same parent as the context node that come before the context node in document order (empty if the context node is an attribute or namespace node).
following	All nodes after the context node in document order, excluding descendants, attributes, and namespace nodes.
preceding	All nodes before the context node in document order, excluding ancestors, attributes, and namespace nodes.
attribute	The attributes of the context node (empty if context node is not an element).
namespace	The namespace nodes of the context node (empty if context node is not an element).
self	Just the context node itself.
descendant-or-self	The context node and descendants of the context node.
ancestor-or-self	The context node and ancestors of the context node.

Node tests

The *node test* part of a step tests each node on the given axis for its name or node type. If a node passes the test, it is included in the resulting node-set. Otherwise, it is filtered out. There are two basic kinds of node test—name tests and node type tests:

- Name tests

  —Wildcard (any name): *

  —Namespace-qualified wildcard (any local name within a particular namespace): xyz:*, abc:*, etc.

  —QName (specific name): foo, xyz:foo, etc.

- Node type tests

  —Any node: node( )

  —Specific type: text( ), comment( ), processing-instruction( )

  —Specific PI target: processing-instruction('foo'), etc.

Name tests only select element nodes, except on the attribute and namespace axes where they only select attributes and namespace nodes, respectively. For example, child::* only returns elements (on the child axis), but attribute::* only returns attributes.

WARNING

One notable consequence of this rule is that self::* will be empty if the context node is not an element node. For example, to select all attributes except those named foo, you might think that this would work: @*[not(self::foo)]. No; name tests on the self axis only select elements. Instead, you will have to use @*[not(local-name( )='foo')].

A QName name test is expanded using the set of namespace/prefix bindings in the XPath expression context. The default namespace of the stylesheet (declared by xmlns) is *not* included in the context. This means that if a QName name test does not include a namespace prefix, then the namespace URI is null, and the name test will only select nodes that are not in a namespace. Conversely, the only way to explicitly select a node whose name is in a namespace is to use a prefix.

TIP

XPath 2.0, unlike XPath 1.0, allows a default namespace declaration (i.e., with an empty prefix) to be a part of the namespace context. And XSLT 2.0's `xpath-default-namespace` attribute is used to declare a default namespace for just that purpose.

Prefixed wildcards (e.g., `xyz:*`) select any node whose name is in the given namespace. As with QName name tests, the namespace URI is derived from the context namespace declarations. For both QNames and prefixed wildcards, it is an error if the name test uses a prefix that is not declared in the expression context.

Use a node type test to select nodes of a particular type, regardless of their name. To select *all* nodes on an axis regardless of their name *or* type, use the `node( )` node test.

Abbreviations

XPath includes some convenient abbreviations, shown in Table 5.

Table 5. XPath abbreviations

Abbreviated form	Non-abbreviated form
.	`self::node( )`
..	`parent::node( )`
@	`attribute::`
//	`/descendant-or-self::node( )/`
foo	`child::foo`

The first two abbreviations in Table 5 are valid expressions by themselves. "." returns the context node, and ".." returns the parent node of the context node. The second two abbreviations are not valid by themselves. "@" must precede a node test. For example, @* selects all attributes of the context node. "//" must precede a step. For example, .//foo selects all descendant foo elements of the context node, and //@* selects all attributes in the same document as the context node.

TIP

Why isn't // just short for /descendant::? The answer is so that it will support expressions like this: //@foo. If // was short for /descendant::, then //@foo would be illegal because it would have two axis specifiers in the same step (descendant and attribute). Instead, // is defined such that //*step* always stands for two distinct steps.

The last abbreviation in Table 5 indicates that child:: is the default axis. In other words, when no axis specifier is included in a step, the child axis is used. For example, foo/bar is equivalent to child::foo/child::bar.

How Location Paths Are Evaluated

As explained earlier in this chapter in the "Steps" section, a step is evaluated by: 1) selecting all the nodes on an axis in relation to a context node, 2) filtering those nodes by using the step's node test, and 3) further filtering the result with one or more optional predicates in the step. That process describes how a single step is evaluated in a single context, i.e., from a single context node.

A location path, however, potentially consists of a sequence of multiple steps, separated by /. A location path is evaluated by iteratively evaluating each step, using each node returned by the sequence of steps to the step's left as the context node for an iteration. The final result of a location path consists of the union of nodes selected by the last step to the right, i.e., the rightmost step in the expression.

For example, `table/tr/td` selects just `td` elements. Specifically, it returns every `td` child of every `tr` child of every `table` child of the context node. The sequence of steps to the left (`table/tr`) of the last step (`td`) determines what nodes to use as context nodes for evaluating `td`. In this case, the `td` step is evaluated as many times as there are `tr` elements; each `tr` element serves as the context node for an evaluation of the `td` step. The final result is the union of the node-sets resulting from those evaluations.

Predicates

A *predicate* is a filter that can be appended to any node-set expression; it is delimited by square brackets (`[...]`). The predicate filters the node-set to produce a new node-set. For each node in the node-set to be filtered, the predicate is evaluated using that node as the context node. If the result is true, then the node is retained in the new node-set. If false, then the node is excluded from the new node-set.

For example, the following predicate filters a step in a location path expression. It filters the node-set returned by the `price` expression:

```
price[. > 20]
```

The expression `price` by itself returns a node-set consisting of all child `price` elements of the context node. The predicate expression `. > 20` serves as a filter on that node-set. For each `price` element, the predicate is evaluated using that element as the context node. If the predicate returns true, then the element is retained. Otherwise, it is filtered from the final result. In this case, the entire expression returns only the child `price` elements whose string-value is a number greater than 20.

Context size in predicates

Not only does the context node change when inside a predicate, but so do the context size and context position. In other words, ., last( ), and position( ) all return different values inside a predicate expression than they would at the top-level context for the XPath expression.

Inside a predicate, the context size is set to the number of nodes in the node-set to be filtered. Each time the predicate is evaluated, the last( ) function consistently returns the same number: the total number of nodes in the node-set being filtered.

Context position in predicates

The context position, however, is different for each node in the node-set to be filtered. Each time the predicate is evaluated, the position( ) function will return a different number. The context position for each node is set to the node's *proximity position* relative to the other nodes in the node-set to be filtered. The proximity position of the node is its position in the node-set ordered either in document order or reverse document order. Which order is used depends on the axis of the step being filtered. If the axis is a *forward axis*, then document order is used. If the axis is a *reverse axis*, then reverse document order is used. The reverse axes are:

```
ancestor
ancestor-or-self
preceding
preceding-sibling
```

All the other axes are forward axes.

Thus, preceding::foo[position( )=3] returns the third preceding foo element, counting *in reverse document order*. Compare it to following::foo[position( )=3], which returns the third following foo element, counting *in document order*. That's because preceding is a reverse axis and following is a forward axis.

Numeric predicates

When a predicate expression does not evaluate directly to a boolean, then it must be converted to a boolean. If the value of the expression before being converted is not a number (e.g., a string or node-set), then it is converted to a boolean as if by calling the `boolean()` function. See the section "Data Type Conversions" in Chapter 5.

However, if the value of the predicate expression before being converted *is* a number, then it is converted to a boolean in a special way: it converts to true if it is equal to the context position, and false otherwise. Effectively, `foo[n]` is shorthand for `foo[position()=n]`. For example, `para[3]` returns the third `para` child element in document order.

"Step filters" versus "expression filters"

There are technically two kinds of predicates. We'll classify them as "step filters" and "expression filters." The difference in behavior arises whenever the predicate tests for context position or context size (using `position()` or `last()`, or a numeric predicate expression as in the following examples). Here is an example step filter:

```
foo/bar[3]
```

In this case, the predicate is a step filter because it is tightly bound to the node test it filters (`bar`), and it affects only the evaluation of the step that it is a part of. The previous expression returns every third `bar` child of every `foo` child of the context node. The resulting node-set may contain more than one `bar` node. On the other hand, the following is an "expression filter" and, in this case, will return, at most, one `bar` node:

```
(foo/bar)[3]
```

The parentheses separate the predicate from the second step and cause it to apply to the entire expression to its left. The filtered expression returns, among all the bar children of the foo children of the context node, just the third child in document order. Other example expression filters are when predicates apply to a function call or variable reference, as in id(foo)[3] or $ns[3].

Whenever an "expression filter" is used, position( ) returns the position of the context node in the node-set ordered *in document order*. Thus, for example, $ns[3] will return the third node in document order among the nodes in $ns. Likewise, (preceding::foo)[3] returns, among all the preceding foo elements, the third preceding element *in document order*. That's because the parentheses cause the predicate to become an "expression filter," which always evaluates position( ) with respect to document order (regardless of any axes used inside the expression).

Other Node-Set Expressions

We've seen how the predicate operator ([...]) can act as an "expression filter" to any node-set expression—whether a function call, variable reference, or parenthesized location path. In addition, the /, //, and | (union) operators can be applied to any node-set expression.

The union operator (|) combines the members of two node-sets. For example, foo | bar selects both the foo and bar child elements of the context node. It's an error if either operand of | doesn't return a node-set.

The / operator and the // abbreviation both compose an expression with a relative location path. The resulting expression is evaluated in the same way that location paths are evaluated. For example, the expression $var/foo returns all foo child elements of the nodes in $var. It's an error if the expression to the left of / or // doesn't return a node-set. Here are some other examples of composing an expression with a location path: id('xyz')/foo and (foo|bar)//foo.

Number Expressions

The XPath number type represents IEEE 754 floating-point numbers, including the special "Not-a-Number" value NaN. Because there is only one number type, the literal 3, for example, is equivalent to the literal 3.0.

TIP

XPath 2.0, in contrast, makes a distinction between integer, decimal, and double literals because it incorporates the built-in simple data types of W3C XML Schema into the language.

Arithmetic Operators

There are six arithmetic operators in XPath 1.0 (five binary and one unary). Listed in order starting from the highest precedence, they are:

- `-` (unary)
- `*`, `div`, `mod`
- `+`, `-`

For example, `(-2 * 5 + 3) mod 2` evaluates to −1. The numeric operators convert their operands to numbers as if by calling the `number()` function. See the "Data Type Conversions" section in Chapter 5.

String Expressions

The only kind of string expression available in XPath 1.0 is a literal string, enclosed in either quotes or apostrophes, as in `"foo"` or `'foo'`. If the string itself contains the quote character (`"`), then it must be delimited by apostrophes, e.g., `'He said, "Hello"'`. Conversely, if it contains an apostrophe (`'`), then it must be delimited by quotes: `"It's her's"`. Because

XPath 1.0 has no character-escaping mechanism, string literals cannot contain both an apostrophe and a quote.

TIP

You can create a string that contains both an apostrophe and a quote by concatenating two literals, e.g., concat("We're saying, ", '"Good bye"'). When using XPath in the context of XSLT, you'll need to XML-escape whichever character is used as the attribute value delimiter, e.g., select="concat("We're saying, ", '"Good bye"')".

String manipulation is done via the string-related functions. See Chapter 5.

Boolean Expressions

There are no boolean literals in XPath, but there are two functions for returning true and false values, namely true( ) and false( ).

XPath contains eight boolean operators (all binary). Listed in order starting from the highest precedence, they are:

- <=, <, >=, >
- =, !=
- and
- or

The and and or operators take two boolean values, converting their operands to booleans if necessary as if by calling the boolean( ) function. In Chapter 5, see the section "Data Type Conversions."

Comparisons Involving Node-Sets

The relational (<=, <, >=, >) and equality (=, !=) operators have special behavior when one or both operands is a node-set. The behavior is partially defined in terms of how simple values are compared. First, we'll go over the rules for comparing node-sets; then, we'll look at how simple values are compared.

When both operands are node-sets, the comparison returns true if there is *any* node in the first node-set and *any* node in the second node-set, such that the result of performing the comparison on the string-values of the two nodes is true. For example, foo=bar returns true if there is any foo child element whose string-value is equal to the string-value of any bar child element. Similarly, foo > bar returns true if there is any foo child element whose string-value after converting it to a number is larger than the string-value of any bar element after converting it to a number.

If one operand is a node-set and the other is a boolean, then the comparison returns true if the result of performing the comparison on the boolean and the result of converting the node-set to a boolean is true. For example, foo=false( ) returns true only if foo returns an empty node-set.

TIP

XPath 2.0 changes the rules for comparing booleans and node-sets, so that such comparisons will behave more like the comparison between node-sets and other types (string or number).

Otherwise, when one operand is a node-set (and the other operand is not a boolean), the comparison returns true if there is *any* node in the node-set, such that the result of performing the comparison on the string-value of the node and the other (string or number) value is true.

All comparisons with an empty node-set return false.

WARNING

For this reason, it is a good idea to get in the habit of using the not( ) function, rather than the != operator, when comparing note-sets.

Comparing Simple Values

The relational operators (<=, <, >=, >) compare numbers only. Both operands are converted to a number. See the section "Data Type Conversions" in Chapter 5.

The equality operators (=, !=) compare booleans, numbers, or strings, depending on the initial type of the operands. If one operand is a boolean, then the other is converted to a boolean as if by calling the boolean( ) function. Otherwise, if one is a number, then the other is converted to a number as if by calling the number( ) function. Otherwise, the operands are compared as strings.

CHAPTER 3

How XSLT Works

XSLT is a language for transforming XML documents. As described in Chapter 1, the XSLT processor is concerned with three XPath data model trees: the source tree, the stylesheet tree, and the result tree. Figure 2 shows the relationship between these three. The stylesheet and source trees are fed to the XSLT processor, which then produces the result tree.

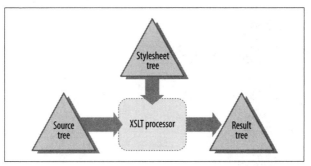

Figure 2. The three trees present in every XSLT transformation

Stylesheet Structure

The general structure of an XSLT stylesheet looks like this:

```
<xsl:stylesheet version="1.0"
  xmlns:xsl="http://www.w3.org/1999/XSL/Transform">
```

```
<!-- optional top-level elements, such as: -->
<xsl:import href="..."/>
<xsl:param name="..."/>

<!-- set of template rules: -->
<xsl:template match="...">...</xsl:template>
<xsl:template match="...">...</xsl:template>
...

</xsl:stylesheet>
```

The document, or root, element of the stylesheet is xsl:
stylesheet. Alternatively, you can use the xsl:transform
element, which behaves exactly the same way. Which you
use is a matter of personal preference. The XSLT namespace
is http://www.w3.org/1999/XSL/Transform. The conventional
namespace prefix is xsl, but any prefix can be used—provided that it binds to the XSLT namespace URI.

See Chapter 4 for a classification of all of XSLT's elements
and where they can occur within a stylesheet.

Processing Model

All XSLT processing consists of iterations over lists of nodes.
At any given point in the execution of a stylesheet there is a
current node for that iteration, and there is a *current node list*
being iterated over. The current node list is the ordered list of
nodes being iterated over, and the current node is a member
of that list.

There are two mechanisms for iterating over a list of nodes:
xsl:apply-templates and xsl:for-each. xsl:apply-templates
is an XSLT instruction that iterates over a given node-set. It
invokes the best-matching *template rule* for each of the nodes
in the node-set. For example, here is an instruction that iterates over the node-set returned by the expression foo:

```
<xsl:apply-templates select="foo"/>
```

The value of the select attribute is an XPath expression that must evaluate to a node-set. The nodes in that set populate the current node list, sorting themselves in document order. Then, for each node in the list, the XSLT processor invokes the best-matching template rule.

Regardless of what your stylesheet contains, XSLT processing always begins with a virtual call to:

```
<xsl:apply-templates select="/"/>
```

This sets the current node list to a list containing only one node—the root node of the source tree. It then invokes the template rule that matches the root node. This virtual call constructs the entire result tree, which, after all, is the point of executing a stylesheet. Your job as an XSLT stylesheet author is to define—using template rules—what happens when the XSLT processor executes this instruction.

Now, let's define what a template rule is.

Template Rules

An XSLT stylesheet contains a set of template rules. Broadly speaking, there are two kinds of template rules:

- Those you define
- Those that XSLT defines for you, a.k.a. the *built-in template rules*

XSLT defines a built-in template rule for each of the seven types of node. This ensures that any call to xsl:apply-templates will never fail to find a matching template rule for the current node, even if your stylesheet contains no explicit template rules at all (an empty stylesheet). We'll define exactly what the built-in template rules are in the "Built-In Template Rules" section later in this chapter.

The template rules that *you* define are explicitly present in your stylesheet. They are xsl:template elements that have a match attribute. Example 1 shows a template rule that matches any foo element.

Example 1. A template rule

```
<xsl:template match="foo">
  <!-- construct part of the result tree -->
  <xsl:apply-templates/>
  ...
</xsl:template>
```

The value of the match attribute is an XSLT *pattern*. Unlike an XPath expression, a pattern is not concerned with selecting a set of nodes from a given context. Instead, it has a more passive role. The above template rule effectively announces "I know how to process foo elements." It will only get invoked when the node being iterated over is a foo element. We'll look more closely at how patterns are interpreted in the upcoming section "Patterns."

Applying Template Rules

Whenever xsl:apply-templates is called, the XSLT processor examines the patterns of all the stylesheet's template rules. For each node being iterated over, it first finds all the template rules with patterns that match the node and then *instantiates* the best-matching template rule among them.

TIP

It is possible to make xsl:apply-templates iterate over a node-set in an order other than document order. See the section "<xsl:sort>" in Chapter 4.

The template rule we saw in Example 1 contained an xsl: apply-templates element. There are two things worth noting about this. First, its presence illustrates the recursive nature of XSLT processing. Starting from the first virtual call to

---

`<xsl:apply-templates select="/"/>`, the recursion continues as long as the `xsl:apply-templates` instruction appears inside an instantiated template rule and is given a nonempty list of nodes to process. This process continues until there are no more nodes to process. At that point, the entire result tree has been constructed.

The second thing worth noting is that the `select` attribute on `xsl:apply-templates` is optional:

```
<xsl:apply-templates/>
```

When absent, it is short for:

```
<xsl:apply-templates select="node( )"/>
```

This instruction applies templates to the child nodes of the current node. In other words, it populates the current node list with the set of nodes returned by the `node( )` expression, and it iterates over them in document order, invoking the best-matching template rule for each node.

TIP

In object oriented (OO) terms, `xsl:apply-templates` is like a function that iterates over a list of objects (nodes) and, for each object, calls the same polymorphic function. Each template rule in your stylesheet defines a different implementation of that single polymorphic function. Which implementation is chosen depends on the runtime characteristics of the object (node). Loosely speaking, you define all the potential bindings by associating a "type" (pattern) with each implementation (template rule).

Patterns

XSLT patterns appear most commonly inside the `xsl:template` element's `match` attribute. (They also appear in certain attributes of the `xsl:key` and `xsl:number` elements.) The allowed syntax for a pattern is a subset of the allowed syntax for XPath expressions. In other words, every pattern is also a syntactically valid expression, but not every expression is a valid pattern.

A pattern consists of one or more *location path patterns* separated by |. A location path pattern is a location path that exclusively uses either the child or attribute axis in each of its steps. The // operator (in its abbreviated form only) can also be used. Finally, a location path pattern can also start with an id( ) or key( ) function call with a literal string argument.

TIP

See Appendix B for a precise EBNF definition for the syntax of patterns.

Here are a few example patterns:

- / matches the root node.
- /doc[@format='simple'] matches the root element only if its name is doc and it has a format attribute with the value simple.
- bar matches any bar element.
- foo/bar matches any bar element whose parent is a foo element.
- id('xyz')/foo matches any foo element whose parent is an element that has an ID-typed attribute with the value xyz.
- section//para matches any para element that has a section element ancestor.
- @foo matches any attribute named foo.
- @* matches any attribute.
- node( ) matches any child node (i.e., element, text, comment, or processing instruction).
- text( ) matches any text node.
- * matches any element.
- xyz:* matches any element in the namespace designated by the xyz prefix.

- `*[not(self::xyz:*)]` matches any element that is *not* in the namespace designated by the xyz prefix.
- `para[2]` matches any para element that is the second para child of its parent.
- `para[last()]` matches any para element that is the last para child of its parent.

Whether a given node matches a pattern may be intuitive, but the precise definition is this:

> A node matches a pattern if the node is a member of the result of evaluating the pattern as an expression with respect to some possible context node.

Because patterns allow only downward-looking axes (child, attribute, and //), the "possible context node" will always be one of the node's ancestors (or the node itself in the case of the pattern "/").

When a pattern consists of more than one location path pattern separated by |, the location path patterns are treated as alternatives. A node matches the pattern if it matches any of the alternatives. The upshot of this is that two or more template rules that have the same content can be syntactically combined into one xsl:template element, simply by putting their match values together and separating them with |. For example, this:

```
<xsl:template match="foo | bar">
  <hi/>
</xsl:template>
```

is short for this:

```
<xsl:template match="foo">
  <hi/>
</xsl:template>

<xsl:template match="bar">
  <hi/>
</xsl:template>
```

Conflict Resolution for Template Rules

When a given node matches the patterns of more than one template rule, the XSLT processor decides which template rule to instantiate according to its rules for conflict resolution. For example, it is quite common to have a stylesheet that includes two template rules like these:

```
<xsl:template match="foo">
  <!-- ... -->
</xsl:template>

<xsl:template match="*">
  <!-- ... -->
</xsl:template>
```

The first template rule matches foo elements. The second matches *any* element. That means that a foo element will match both template rules. But the XSLT processor has to pick only one of them. Assuming that the stylesheet containing these rules isn't imported into another stylesheet that overrides them, the XSLT processor will pick the template rule with the foo pattern. Based on a comparison of the patterns * and foo, it determines that foo has higher *priority*. Generally speaking, the more specific a pattern is, the higher priority it has. We'll describe exactly how priority is determined in the next section, "Priority."

However, before patterns are ever examined for their relative priority, the XSLT processor first eliminates all matching template rules that have lower *import precedence*. Basically, template rules in an imported stylesheet have lower import precedence than template rules in the importing stylesheet. For the precise rules on how import precedence is determined, see the "<xsl:import>" section in Chapter 4.

Thus, there are two steps in this process of elimination:

1. The XSLT processor eliminates rules with *lower import precedence*.
2. Among the remaining template rules, the XSLT processor eliminates the rules with *lower priority*.

It is an error if there is more than one template rule left. If that happens, the XSLT processor can either signal the error or recover by invoking the matching template rule that occurs last in the stylesheet. Most processors will at least give a warning if this happens.

TIP

It is also possible to invoke an imported template rule that has been overridden. See the "<xsl:apply-imports>" section in Chapter 4.

Priority

A template rule can explicitly specify its priority using the optional priority attribute on the xsl:template element. The value of the priority attribute may be any decimal number—positive or negative. The higher the number in the priority attribute, the higher the priority of the template rule.

If the priority attribute is absent (which is most often the case), then the template rule assumes a *default priority* based on the format of its pattern, i.e., the format of the match attribute's value. If the pattern consists of multiple location path patterns separated by |, then the multiple alternatives are considered to be separate template rules for purposes of assigning a default priority. There are four default priority values: -.5, -.25, 0, and .5. All location path patterns can be classified into one of these four default priority values, as shown in Table 6.

Table 6. Default priorities for location path patterns

Default priority	Format of location path pattern	Examples
-.5	Name test wildcard (any name), or node type test (regardless of name)	* @* node( ) text( ) comment( ) processing-instruction( )

Table 6. Default priorities for location path patterns (continued)

Default priority	Format of location path pattern	Examples
-.25	Namespace-qualified wildcard (regardless of local name)	`xyz:*` `@xyz:*`

0	Name test for a particular name, or `processing-instruction(`*Literal*`)`	`foo`
		`xyz:foo`
		`@foo`
		`@xyz:foo`
		`processing-instruction('foo')`

.5	Any other location path pattern. In other words, any one that includes any of these operators: /, //, or [ ]	`/`
		`/foo`
		`foo/bar`
		`foo[2]`
		`/foo[bar='bat']`

Modes

Both the `xsl:template` and `xsl:apply-templates` elements can have an optional mode attribute. Modes let you partition sets of template rules into different independent scopes. For example, this instruction will only consider template rules associated with the foo mode:

```
<xsl:apply-templates mode="foo"/>
```

And here is an example template rule that's associated with the foo mode:

```
<xsl:template match="*" mode="foo">
  <!-- ... -->
</xsl:template>
```

If you leave the mode attribute off of `xsl:apply-templates`, then only the template rules that have no mode attribute will be considered. This is considered to be the unnamed, or default, mode.

Modes effectively allow you to define different template rules for the same node. In other words, you can process the same node two different times and do something different each time. A common use case for modes is generating a table of contents. Most of your template rules in a stylesheet might be concerned with generating the document content (headings, paragraphs, etc.) like this:

```
<xsl:template match="heading">
  <h1>
    <xsl:value-of select="."/>
  </h1>
</xsl:template>
```

However, to generate entries for a table of contents, you could define corresponding template rules in the toc mode:

```
<xsl:template match="heading" mode="toc">
  <li>
    <xsl:value-of select="."/>
  </li>
</xsl:template>
```

For heading elements, `<xsl:apply-templates/>` will generate h1 elements, and `<xsl:apply-templates mode="toc"/>` will generate li elements.

TIP

Furthering the OO analogy, a mode name identifies *which* polymorphic function to execute repeatedly in a call to xsl:apply-templates. (See the second Tip in the "Applying Template Rules" section earlier in this chapter.) When mode="foo" is set, foo acts as the name of a polymorphic function, and each template rule with mode="foo" defines an implementation of the foo function.

Built-In Template Rules

By definition, the built-in template rules have lower import precedence than any template rules that you explicitly define. Thus, explicit template rules always override built-in template rules. The built-in rules come in handy when you don't specify an explicit template rule to match a particular node.

The built-in template rule for root nodes and element nodes is to apply templates to children. The explicit formulation of this rule is:

```
<xsl:template match="/|*">
  <xsl:apply-templates/>
</xsl:template>
```

TIP

Many stylesheets include an explicit template rule that matches the root node: `<xsl:template match="/">`.... This allows you to take control of processing right off the bat; however, it isn't required. Instead, you could rely on the built-in template rule for root nodes and elements to recursively apply templates until they reach a node for which you *have* defined an explicit template rule.

For each mode that's used in a stylesheet, XSLT also automatically defines an equivalent built-in template rule for root nodes and elements that automates continued processing of children within the same mode:

```
<xsl:template match="/|*" mode="mode-name">
  <xsl:apply-templates mode="mode-name"/>
</xsl:template>
```

The built-in template rule for text nodes and attribute nodes is to create a text node with the string-value of the node. The explicit formulation of this rule is:

```
<xsl:template match="text()|@*">
  <xsl:value-of select="."/>
</xsl:template>
```

TIP

The net effect of this rule is that text nodes, by default, are copied to the result tree. This is evident if you try executing an empty stylesheet—an xsl:stylesheet element that contains no explicit template rules. The result tree consists of one large text node—a concatenation of all text nodes in the source tree.

The built-in template rule for processing instructions and comments is to do nothing:

```
<xsl:template match="processing-instruction()|comment()"/>
```

The built-in template rule for namespace nodes is also to do nothing. Since no pattern can match a namespace node, there is no explicit formulation of this rule, and it cannot be overridden.

Template Rule Content

When an XSLT processor invokes a template rule, it *instantiates* the contents of the template rule, thereby constructing part of the result tree. The content of the xsl:template element (following zero or more optional xsl:param elements) is a "template" for constructing part of the result tree. This "template" can contain both elements and text. Elements in the XSLT namespace are called *instructions*, elements in an extension namespace are called *extension elements*, and elements in any other namespace (or no namespace) are called *literal result elements*.

TIP

See Chapter 6 for more information on extension elements.

A text node acts as an instruction to create a corresponding text node in the result tree. In other words, text nodes in the stylesheet are copied to the result tree automatically.

TIP

This is *not* normally the case for whitespace-only text nodes in the stylesheet. See the "Whitespace Stripping" section later in this chapter.

Comments and processing instructions in the stylesheet are ignored. To create those, you must use the corresponding XSLT instruction for doing so.

Literal Result Elements

A literal result element acts as an instruction to construct an element node with the same name in the result tree. The XSLT processor effectively creates a shallow copy of the literal result element from the stylesheet and inserts it into the result tree at the location within the result tree that is currently being constructed.

Attributes that appear on literal result elements, except for attributes in the XSLT namespace, are also copied to the result tree, attached to the corresponding element in the result tree. For example, this template rule creates an order element with a num attribute:

```
<xsl:template match="...">
  <order num="123-987">
    <!-- ... -->
  </order>
</xsl:template>
```

Each time this template rule gets instantiated, the order element is copied shallowly to the result tree along with its num attribute. The content of the order element in the result tree is the result of instantiating the content of the order element in the stylesheet.

Attribute Value Templates

Attributes on literal result elements are interpreted as *attribute value templates* (AVTs). This means that you can use curly braces ({...}) to insert a dynamically computed value into the attribute value. For example, here is a modification of the previous example:

```
<order num="{$prefix}-987">
  <!-- ... -->
</order>
```

The curly braces within the attribute delimit an XPath expression evaluated in the current XSLT context. In this case, the expression is a variable reference. The $prefix expression is evaluated, and in place of {$prefix}, the value of the expression after converting it to a string appears in the result. For example, if $prefix evaluates to the string (or number) 555, then the result would look like this: <order name="555-987"/>.

In addition to the attributes of literal result elements, some attributes of elements in the XSLT namespace are interpreted as AVTs. In other words, the curly braces ({...}) have the special significance just illustrated. In either case, if you want to include an actual brace character in the resulting attribute value, you can escape it by repeating the brace. In an AVT context, {{ is the escape sequence for {, and }} is the escape sequence for }.

How XPath Context Is Initialized

Many XSLT instructions have XPath expressions in their attributes, e.g., the respective select attributes of xsl:value-of, xsl:copy-of, xsl:for-each, and xsl:apply-templates. XPath expressions may also, of course, appear inside attribute value templates. As far as XSLT processing goes, an XPath expression is a black box that yields a value—a node-set, number, string, boolean, or result tree fragment. However, as noted in the previous chapter, all XPath expressions are evaluated in a context. The current node and current node list supply an important part of that context, as shown in Table 7.

Table 7. How XSLT initializes XPath expression context

Context component	Set to:
Context node	The current node
Context size	The number of nodes in the current node list (1 or greater)
Context position	The position of the current node in the current node list (1 or greater)
Namespace declarations	The namespace declarations in scope for the element whose attribute contains the expression (excluding any default namespace declarations)
Variable bindings	The variable bindings in scope for the element whose attribute contains the expression
Function library	The built-in XPath/XSLT functions, in addition to any extension functions that are available

The current node and current node list remain the same throughout the content of a given template rule—with one important exception. XSLT's other mechanism for iterating over a list of nodes, the xsl:for-each instruction, also changes the current node and current node list. Like xsl:apply-templates, xsl:for-each iterates over a given node-set in document order (by default). But rather than dispatching the behavior for each node to a template rule, it instantiates the content of the xsl:for-each element itself—the same content for every node in the list.

For example, the following template rule includes several relative XPath expressions. The context node for each expression depends on what the current node is in XSLT processing:

```
<xsl:template match="order">
  <!-- current node is an "order" element -->
  <p>Order: <xsl:value-of select="number"/></p>
  <xsl:for-each select="item">
    <!-- current node changes to an "item" element -->
    <p>Item: <xsl:value-of select="name"/></p>
  </xsl:for-each>
  <!-- current node changes back to the "order" element -->
  <p>Total: <xsl:value-of select="total"/></p>
</xsl:template>
```

The number, item, and total expressions are evaluated with an order element as the context node. However, the expression name is evaluated with an item element as the context node. That's because the current node, and thus the XPath context node, changes as processing enters the xsl:for-each instruction and changes back after it completes. Thus, the document that this template rule is designed to process probably has a structure like this:

```
<order>
  <number>123</number>
  <total>$34.95</total>
  <item>
    <name>Widget</name>
  </item>
  <item>
    <name>Dingbat</name>
  </item>
  ...
</order>
```

"Current node" and "context node" refer to the same node, except inside predicates. Inside a predicate, the context node changes for each evaluation of the predicate expression. "Current node," however, is an XSLT term and refers to the outer context node of the entire expression. XSLT provides a function specifically for the purpose of accessing the current node from inside a predicate expression. See the current( ) function in Chapter 5.

Whitespace Stripping

Whitespace-only text nodes in an XSLT stylesheet are considered insignificant and are stripped from the stylesheet tree before XSLT processing begins—except when they occur inside xsl:text elements or elements with the declaration xml:space="preserve". See the "<xsl:text>" section in the next chapter.

Whitespace stripping is also an optional process that can be applied to the source tree before XSLT processing begins. By default, unlike the stylesheet tree, all whitespace is preserved in the source tree. See the sections "<xsl:strip-space>" and "<xsl:preserve-space>" in the next chapter.

Serializing the Result Tree

XSLT processing is primarily concerned with constructing a result tree. Serialization involves converting that result tree to an actual XML stream or file. The xsl:output element is a top-level element that lets you give hints to the XSLT processor about how you want your result tree to be serialized. Technically, the XSLT processor is not required to heed the hints you give it (or even to serialize the result tree at all), but if it does heed your hints, it must follow the rules for interpreting the xsl:output element. See the "<xsl:output>" section in the next chapter.

Disabling Output Escaping

The xsl:value-of and xsl:text instructions have an optional attribute named disable-output-escaping, whose value must be yes or no. The default value is no. When the value is yes, the XSLT processor disables the normal escaping of markup characters in the value of the text node when it serializes the result. For example, consider this instruction:

```
<xsl:text disable-output-escaping="yes">&lt;</xsl:text>
```

The above instruction will output a literal < character in the result instead of its normal escaped representation (<).

You should rarely, if ever, use the disable-output-escaping attribute. Quoting the XSLT recommendation itself:

> Since disabling output escaping may not work with all XSLT processors and can result in XML that is not well-formed, it should be used only when there is no alternative.

XSLT Elements by Use Case

The next chapter contains a reference for all of the XSLT elements. Table 8 shows a list of general programming use cases and the corresponding XSLT elements that you should refer to in that chapter. If you don't already know what you're looking for, this table can serve as a map.

Table 8. Basic programming use cases in XSLT

Use case	Relevant XSLT elements
Creating nodes	xsl:element, xsl:attribute, xsl:text, xsl:comment, xsl:processing-instruction
Copying nodes	xsl:copy-of, xsl:copy
Repetition (looping)	xsl:for-each
Sorting	xsl:sort
Conditional processing	xsl:choose, xsl:if
Computing or extracting a value	xsl:value-of
Defining variables and parameters	xsl:variable, xsl:param
Defining and calling subprocedures (named templates)	xsl:template, xsl:call-template
Defining and applying template rules	xsl:template, xsl:apply-templates, xsl:apply-imports
Numbering and number formatting	xsl:number, xsl:decimal-format
Debugging	xsl:message
Combining stylesheets (modularization)	xsl:import, xsl:include
Compatibility	xsl:fallback
Building lookup indexes	xsl:key
XSLT code generation	xsl:namespace-alias
Output formatting	xsl:output
Whitespace stripping	xsl:strip-space, xsl:preserve-space

CHAPTER 4

Elements

This chapter contains an alphabetical reference of the elements in the XSLT namespace (http://www.w3.org/1999/XSL/Transform) that are a part of XSLT 1.0. Some of these elements are *instructions*; some are *top-level* elements. Others don't fall into either category, so we'll call them "special."

TIP

The names of XSLT elements in this chapter include the conventional xsl prefix. Of course, any prefix could be used as long as it binds to the XSLT namespace.

Top-Level Elements

A *top-level element* is an element that occurs as the child of the stylesheet's document element (either xsl:stylesheet or xsl:transform). Below are all the top-level XSLT elements, listed in alphabetical order:

xsl:attribute-set	xsl:output
xsl:decimal-format	xsl:param
xsl:import	xsl:preserve-space
xsl:include	xsl:strip-space
xsl:key	xsl:template
xsl:namespace-alias	xsl:variable

These elements may occur in any order, except for one important exception: any xsl:import elements, if present, must come first, before all other top-level elements.

Instructions

An *instruction* is any XSLT element that can occur in the context of a "template," which is what the XSLT 1.0 spec calls code that creates part of the result tree (or, when inside xsl:variable, a *result tree fragment* that may or may not be copied into the final result tree). Instructions are usually interleaved with *literal result elements* and their attributes. Literal result elements are elements that are not in the XSLT namespace. Here are all the XSLT instructions, listed in alphabetical order:

xsl:apply-imports	xsl:fallback
xsl:apply-templates	xsl:for-each
xsl:attribute	xsl:if
xsl:call-template	xsl:message
xsl:choose	xsl:number
xsl:comment	xsl:processing-instruction
xsl:copy	xsl:text
xsl:copy-of	xsl:value-of
xsl:element	xsl:variable

TIP

Among the XSLT instructions, xsl:variable is unique in that it also may occur as a top-level element.

The most common "template" context is, naturally, the content of the xsl:template element, which means that any of the instructions may occur as children of xsl:template. There are many other "template" contexts—the content of literal result elements, some top-level elements, special elements, and many of the instructions themselves. For example, xsl:for-each can be nested inside itself because it also represents a "template" context. The comprehensive set of "template" contexts can be gleaned from the element reference later in this chapter, which describes the content model of each XSLT element.

TIP

In XSLT 2.0, a series of instructions is called a "sequence constructor" rather than "template." This terminology is more consistent with 2.0's sequence-oriented model, and it also avoids any confusion around the overloaded term "template."

Special Elements

Here are all the elements that don't fit into the other two categories; they represent "special" elements that have unique rules about where they may occur:

```
xsl:otherwise          xsl:transform
xsl:param              xsl:when
xsl:sort               xsl:with-param
xsl:stylesheet
```

For the sake of completeness, here are the corresponding rules for where these elements may occur:

- xsl:stylesheet and xsl:transform are interchangeable names for the document element of an XSLT stylesheet.

- xsl:when and xsl:otherwise may only occur as children of the xsl:choose instruction; the optional xsl:otherwise element must come last.

- xsl:sort elements may occur only as children of xsl: apply-templates or xsl:for-each; when inside xsl:for-each, they must come first.

- `xsl:with-param` elements may occur only as children of `xsl:apply-templates` or `xsl:call-template`.

- `xsl:param` elements may occur only as the first children of `xsl:template`.

TIP

Among the special elements, `xsl:param` is unique in that it may also occur as a top-level element.

QNames

The names of internal XSLT objects are specified as *QNames*. Chapter 2 explained that QName name tests in an XPath expression are expanded using the in-scope namespace declarations, with the exception that a default namespace declaration is *not* used (i.e., a namespace declaration with no prefix, declared by `xmlns`). Internal XSLT object names are expanded according to these same rules; i.e., default namespace declarations are not considered. To put one of these object names in a namespace, you would need to use a prefix. Here are the objects in XSLT whose names are specified as QNames:

Named templates	Keys
Modes	Decimal formats
Attribute sets	Variables and parameters

Element Reference

This section enumerates all the elements in the XSLT namespace that are a part of XSLT 1.0. The valid syntax of each element, including its attributes and content, is described using the notation provided in Appendix B of the XSLT Recommendation (*http://www.w3.org/TR/xslt#element-syntax-summary*).

Attribute names in bold type represent required attributes. All other attributes are optional.

The attribute value placeholder for each attribute describes the allowed format of its value, e.g., *node-set-expression* or *qname*. An attribute value placeholder that has curly braces ({ }) around it means that the attribute is interpreted as an *attribute value template*. See the section "Attribute Value Templates" in Chapter 3.

The content model of each element is described in a comment inside the element. An empty element means that the element must always be empty.

\<xsl:apply-imports\>

```
<xsl:apply-imports/>
```

The xsl:apply-imports instruction applies templates to the current node in the *current template rule*'s mode, taking into consideration only the template rules that were imported into the stylesheet containing the current template rule. It is illegal for xsl:apply-imports to occur as a descendant of xsl:for-each since the *current template rule* property is considered to be set to null when an xsl:for-each element is instantiated.

For example, a stylesheet called *top.xsl* contains the following elements:

```
<xsl:import href="imported.xsl"/>

<xsl:template match="footnote" mode="misc">
  <br/>
  <xsl:apply-imports/>
</xsl:template>
```

And a stylesheet that it imports, called *imported.xsl*, contains this template rule:

```
<xsl:template match="footnote" mode="misc">
  <b>
    <xsl:value-of select="."/>
  </b>
</xsl:template>
```

When templates are first applied to a footnote element in the misc mode, only the matching template rule in *top.xsl* is considered because it has higher import precedence than the matching template rule in *imported.xsl*. However, xsl:apply-imports instructs the XSLT processor to once again apply templates to the current node (footnote) in the same mode (misc), only this time ignoring the current template rule and considering only the template rules that were overridden. In this case, the net effect is that a br element is inserted before the result of the overridden template rule:

```
<br/>
<b>...</b>
```

In this way, a template rule can be overridden but also reused within the template rule that overrides it.

TIP

XSLT 2.0 introduces the xsl:next-match instruction, which provides even greater power for invoking overridden template rules. It considers not only imported template rules, but also template rules with lower priority than the current template rule.

<xsl:apply-templates>

```
<xsl:apply-templates
  select = node-set-expression
  mode = qname>
  <!-- Content: (xsl:sort | xsl:with-param)* -->
</xsl:apply-templates>
```

The xsl:apply-templates instruction applies templates to each of the nodes selected by the node-set expression in its select attribute. If the select attribute is absent, then it defaults to the expression node( ), which selects all child nodes of the current node.

The mode attribute restricts the considered template rules to those in the given mode, i.e., only those xsl:template elements that have a mode attribute with the same value as the mode attribute of the xsl:apply-templates instruction. When the mode attribute is absent, then only those template rules in the unnamed default mode are considered, i.e., only those xsl:template elements that do not have a mode attribute (but that do have a match attribute).

By default, xsl:apply-templates iterates over the supplied node-set in document order. The order can be changed by placing one or more xsl:sort elements inside the xsl:apply-templates instruction. See "<xsl:sort>" later in this chapter.

The xsl:apply-templates instruction may also contain one or more xsl:with-param elements for passing named parameters to the invoked template rules. See "<xsl:with-param>" later in this chapter.

This example's use of the xsl:apply-templates instruction is quite common:

```
<xsl:apply-templates/>
```

It applies templates to all children of the current node, considering only the template rules in the unnamed default mode.

Here's one more example that uses all the allowed syntax features of the instruction:

```
<xsl:apply-templates select="*" mode="chart">
  <xsl:sort select="@size" data-type="number"/>
  <xsl:with-param name="format" select="'alternate'"/>
</xsl:apply-templates>
```

It applies templates in the chart mode to the child elements (*) of the current node, sorting them by the numeric value of their size attributes and passing to each template rule a parameter named format that has the string value alternate.

`<xsl:attribute>`

```
<xsl:attribute
  name = { qname }
  namespace = { uri-reference }>
  <!-- Content: template -->
</xsl:attribute>
```

The `xsl:attribute` instruction adds an attribute to the containing result element, whether created by `xsl:element` or a literal result element. The expanded-name of the resulting attribute is determined by the required `name` attribute and an optional `namespace` attribute. The local part of the `name` attribute's QName value (the name minus the optional prefix) is used as the local name of the resulting attribute.

How the namespace of the resulting attribute is determined depends on whether the `namespace` attribute is present. When present, its value is used as the namespace of the resulting attribute. When absent, the QName value of the `name` attribute is expanded using the in-scope namespace bindings for the `xsl:attribute` element (*not* including any default namespace declaration). The resulting expanded-name is used as the expanded-name of the newly created attribute.

WARNING

Since it is an error to add an attribute to an element after children have been added to it, you must make sure that `xsl:attribute` comes before any child elements, text nodes, etc. Otherwise, the XSLT processor may recover silently from the error by ignoring the `xsl:attribute` instruction.

Here is an example use of the `xsl:attribute` instruction:

```
<xsl:attribute name="style">display:none;</xsl:attribute>
```

Since both the `name` and `namespace` attributes are interpreted as *attribute value templates*, this is also a valid example:

```
<xsl:attribute name="{@name}" namespace="{@uri}">
    foo</xsl:attribute>
```

\<xsl:attribute-set>

```
<xsl:attribute-set
  name = qname
  use-attribute-sets = qnames>
  <!-- Content: xsl:attribute* -->
</xsl:attribute-set>
```

The xsl:attribute-set element is a top-level element that declares a named attribute set, which lets you use the same set of attributes in more than one place in a stylesheet. The required name attribute identifies the attribute set by expanding its QName value. The content of the xsl:attribute-set element consists of a sequence of xsl:attribute elements that make up the attributes in the set. The optional use-attribute-sets attribute enables an attribute set to be composed additionally of other named attribute sets in the stylesheet. Its value is a whitespace-separated list of attribute set names. The attributes from other attribute sets are treated as if they're added, in the order the attribute sets are named, before all the attributes in the set that uses them. If there are duplicate attributes with the same expanded-name in the resulting set, then the last attribute declared replaces any duplicate attributes declared previously.

An attribute set is used either by adding the use-attribute-sets attribute to an xsl:element or xsl:copy instruction, or by adding the xsl:use-attribute-sets attribute to a literal result element. The effect in either case is that attributes in the set are added to the resulting element, just as if the xsl:attribute instructions had been physically copied to that location in the stylesheet. The name, namespace, and value of each attribute in the set are evaluated in the same context as the containing element, with one exception: the only variable bindings that are visible are those in the context of the xsl:attribute-set element itself, i.e., top-level variables and parameters.

Duplicate attributes with the same expanded-name are treated the same way as with duplicates resulting from an attribute set using another attribute set; i.e., the last one declared overrides an earlier duplicate. However, when a literal result element has literal attributes attached to it, those override any attributes with the same expanded-name that are added to the element using xsl:use-attribute-sets.

\<xsl:call-template\>

```
<xsl:call-template
  name = qname>
  <!-- Content: xsl:with-param* -->
</xsl:call-template>
```

The xsl:call-template instruction instantiates a particular xsl:template element identified by name. It is an error if there are no xsl:template elements with a name attribute having the given expanded-name. Parameter values may be passed to a template using one or more nested xsl:with-param elements. See "\<xsl:with-param\>."

Unlike xsl:apply-templates, the xsl:call-template instruction does not change the current node and current node list. For example, consider xsl:call-template:

```
<xsl:template match="para">
  <xsl:call-template name="do-para"/>
</xsl:template>
```

It instantiates the do-para named template:

```
<xsl:template name="do-para">
  <xsl:value-of select="."/>
</xsl:template>
```

The xsl:value-of instruction inside this named template will output the value of the para element because it is still the current node, represented by the XPath expression ".".

\<xsl:choose\>

```
<xsl:choose>
  <!-- Content: (xsl:when+, xsl:otherwise?) -->
</xsl:choose>
```

The xsl:choose instruction selects among one or more conditional branches of execution. It is XSLT's version of an if-else statement. It must contain one or more xsl:when elements, followed by an optional xsl:otherwise element. Each xsl:when element has a test attribute containing an XPath expression that is interpreted as a boolean. The content of the first xsl:when element whose test expression returns true is instantiated, and the remaining branches are ignored. If none of the test expressions return true, then the content of the xsl:otherwise element, if present, is instantiated. If none are true and xsl:otherwise is absent, then nothing is created.

For example:

```
<xsl:choose>
  <xsl:when test="$format='normal'">
    ...
  </xsl:when>
  <xsl:when test="$format='alternate'">
    ...
  </xsl:when>
  <xsl:otherwise>
    ...
  </xsl:otherwise>
</xsl:choose>
```

In this case, which branch is instantiated depends on the value of the $format variable. If it is not equal to normal or alternate, then the content of xsl:otherwise is instantiated.

<xsl:comment>

```
<xsl:comment>
  <!-- Content: template -->
</xsl:comment>
```

The xsl:comment instruction creates a comment node in the result tree. The content of the xsl:comment element is a template for the string-value of the comment node. It is an error to create any kind of node other than a text node inside xsl:comment. Also, the comment text must not contain the string "--".

For example:

```
<xsl:comment>This comment will appear in the result tree
   </xsl:comment>
```

This instruction will create this comment in the result:

```
<!--This comment will appear in the result tree
   -->
```

<xsl:copy>

```
<xsl:copy
  use-attribute-sets = qnames>
  <!-- Content: template -->
</xsl:copy>
```

The xsl:copy instruction makes a copy of the current node. It is most useful when the current node is an element node. Rather than creating a full copy of the element (as with xsl:copy-of), xsl:copy creates a "shallow" copy—an element with the same expanded-name, including the original element's namespace nodes. However, the children and attributes of the original element are excluded. Instead, the template content of the xsl:copy element determines what attributes and children the copied element will have.

When the current node is a text node, comment, processing instruction, attribute, or namespace node, <xsl:copy/> acts the same as <xsl:copy-of select="."/>, and if xsl:copy contains any template content, it is ignored. When the current node is a root node, the opposite happens. Only the template content of xsl:copy is instantiated; since the result tree's root node is created automatically, it does not need to be explicitly copied, so the xsl:copy start and end tags are effectively ignored.

The optional use-attribute-sets attribute is used when copying element nodes only. See "<xsl:attribute-set>" earlier in this chapter.

A common example use of the xsl:copy instruction is as a part of the identity transformation template rule, shown here:

```
<xsl:template match="@*|node( )">
  <xsl:copy>
    <xsl:apply-templates select="@*|node( )"/>
  </xsl:copy>
</xsl:template>
```

This template rule matches attributes and child nodes (elements, comments, processing instructions, and text nodes). It recursively copies element nodes by making a shallow copy of the element and then applying templates to all of its attributes and children. When the current node is not an element, it is simply copied to the result, and the xsl:apply-templates instruction is ignored.

\<xsl:copy-of\>

```
<xsl:copy-of
  select = expression/>
```

The xsl:copy-of instruction performs a deep copy of each of the nodes in the select expression node-set, in document order. A deep copy includes all of the node's children, attributes, and namespace nodes. If the select expression is a variable reference whose value is a result tree fragment, then it is treated as if it were a node-set containing one root node, and the entire fragment is copied to the result.

If the select expression returns a value of a different data type (e.g., number or boolean), then the value is converted to a string and copied to the result. In such cases, xsl:copy-of behaves no differently than the xsl:value-of instruction.

\<xsl:decimal-format\>

```
<xsl:decimal-format
  name = qname
  decimal-separator = char
  grouping-separator = char
```

```
infinity = string
minus-sign = char
NaN = string
percent = char
per-mille = char
zero-digit = char
digit = char
pattern-separator = char />
```

The xsl:decimal-format element is a top-level element that declares a decimal format that configures the behavior of the format-number() function. The name attribute identifies the decimal format and is referenced by the third argument of the format-number() function. If the name attribute is absent, then the element defines the default decimal format for this transformation.

We can classify the rest of the attributes on the xsl:decimal-format element into three categories:

- Those that specify characters that may appear in the result of formatting the number
- Those that control the interpretation of characters in the format pattern
- Those that do both of the above

The following attributes specify characters or strings that may appear in the resulting formatted number:

infinity
    Specifies the string used to represent infinity. Default is Infinity.

NaN
    Specifies the string used to represent NaN. Default is NaN.

minus-sign
    Specifies the character used as the default minus sign. Default is the hyphen-minus character (#x2D).

The following attributes control the interpretation of characters in the format pattern:

digit

Specifies the character used for a digit in the format pattern. Default is the number sign (#).

pattern-separator

Specifies the character used to separate positive and negative sub-patterns in the format pattern. Default is the semicolon (;).

The following attributes both control the interpretation of characters in the format pattern and specify characters that may appear in the result of formatting the number:

decimal-separator

Specifies the character used for the decimal sign. Default is the period (.).

grouping-separator

Specifies the character used for grouping (e.g., thousands). Default is the comma (,).

percent

Specifies the character used as a percent sign. Default is the percent character (%).

per-mille

Specifies the character used as a per mille sign. Default is the Unicode per mille character (#x2030).

zero-digit

Specifies the character used as the digit zero. Default is the digit zero (0).

For example, given this decimal format declaration:

```
<xsl:decimal-format name="alternate"
  decimal-separator=","
  grouping-separator="."/>
```

and this `format-number()` invocation:

```
format-number(10000.123, '#.##0,00', 'alternate')
```

the following string will be returned: `10.000,12`.

Here's another example that uses the default decimal format and outputs a currency value:

```
format-number(5242.1, '$#,##0.00')
```

This example returns the following string:

```
$5,242.10
```

TIP

The XSLT 1.0 recommendation defers the particular rules for how the format pattern string is interpreted to the JDK 1.1 specification. To remove that dependency on an old Java spec, the XSLT 2.0 specification defines the particular (virtually unchanged) rules itself.

See also "<xsl:number>," which has its own distinct number formatting functionality, later in this chapter.

<xsl:element>

```
<xsl:element
  name = { qname }
  namespace = { uri-reference }
  use-attribute-sets = qnames>
  <!-- Content: template -->
</xsl:element>
```

The `xsl:element` instruction creates an element node. The expanded-name of the resulting element is determined by the required `name` attribute and an optional `namespace` attribute. The local part of the `name` attribute's QName value (the name minus the optional prefix) is used as the local name of the resulting element.

How the namespace of the resulting element is determined depends on whether the `namespace` attribute is present. When present, its value is used as the namespace of the resulting element. When absent, the QName value of the `name` attribute is expanded using the in-scope namespace bindings for the `xsl:element` element, *including* any default namespace declaration. The resulting expanded-name is used as the expanded-name of the newly created element.

The optional `use-attribute-sets` attribute causes one or more sets of attributes to be created on the resulting element. See "<xsl:attribute-set>."

Here is an example use of the `xsl:element` instruction:

```
<xsl:element name="div">...</xsl:attribute>
```

This is equivalent to using a literal result element:

```
<div>...</div>
```

The `xsl:element` instruction is most useful when you need to compute the name of the element at runtime, which is not possible with a literal result element. It is possible with `xsl:element` because both the `name` and `namespace` attributes are interpreted as *attribute value templates*. For example, to effectively make a shallow copy of an element without copying any of its namespace nodes (which is what happens with `xsl:copy`), you can use the `xsl:element` instruction to create a new element node having the same name and namespace URI:

```
<xsl:element name="{name( )}"
    namespace="{namespace-uri( )}">...</xsl:element>
```

<xsl:fallback>

```
<xsl:fallback>
  <!-- Content: template -->
</xsl:fallback>
```

The xsl:fallback instruction provides an alternate implementation of the parent instruction in the event that the parent instruction is not recognized by the XSLT processor. This is possible either because the XSLT instruction is from a future version of XSLT or because the element is an extension element for which the XSLT processor does not have an implementation.

The xsl:fallback element is instantiated only when the parent instruction element is not recognized.

For example, the following stylesheet is designed to be portable between XSLT 2.0 processors, XSLT 1.0 processors that support the EXSLT extensions, and Xalan. It provides three possible instructions for multiple output documents: XSLT 2.0's xsl:result-document, EXSLT's exsl:document, and Xalan's redirect:write extension.

```
<xsl:stylesheet version="2.0"
  xmlns:xsl="http://www.w3.org/1999/XSL/Transform"
  xmlns:exsl="http://exslt.org/common"
  xmlns:redirect="http://xml.apache.org/xalan/redirect"
  extension-element-prefixes="exsl redirect">

  <xsl:template match="/">
    <xsl:result-document href="output.xml">
      <xsl:call-template name="do-document"/>
      <xsl:fallback>
        <exsl:document href="output.xml">
          <xsl:call-template name="do-document"/>
          <xsl:fallback>
            <redirect:write file="output.xml">
              <xsl:call-template name="do-document"/>
            </redirect:write>
          </xsl:fallback>
        </exsl:document>
      </xsl:fallback>
    </xsl:result-document>
  </xsl:template>
</xsl:stylesheet>
```

```
<xsl:template name="do-document">
  <foo/>
</xsl:template>

</xsl:stylesheet>
```

In the event that this is a 1.0 processor, it will not recognize the xsl:result-document instruction and will instantiate the nested xsl:fallback instruction instead. If it, in turn, does not implement the exsl:document extension, then it will try to instantiate the redirect:write extension element. If it does not recognize that element either, then it will finally throw an error because there is no fallback provided for that scenario.

You can also perform fallback processing with the element-available( ) function and conditional processing. See the element-available( ) function in Chapter 5.

<xsl:for-each>

```
<xsl:for-each
  select = node-set-expression>
  <!-- Content: (xsl:sort*, template) -->
</xsl:for-each>
```

The xsl:for-each instruction iterates over each of the nodes in the node-set returned by the expression in its select attribute. By default, it iterates over them in document order. One or more nested xsl:sort elements can change the ordering. See "<xsl:sort>."

The template content of the xsl:for-each instruction is instantiated once for each node in the node-set. Like xsl:apply-templates, xsl:for-each changes the *current node* and *current node list* context. Each node in the node-set in turn becomes the current node, and the entire node-set becomes the current node list.

For example, this instruction iterates over the set of order child elements of the current node outside the xsl:for-each element.

```
<xsl:for-each select="order">
  <br/>
  The phone number for this order is <xsl:value-of select=
    "phone"/>.
</xsl:for-each>
```

Inside the xsl:for-each element, however, the current node changes. Each of the order elements being iterated over takes its turn as the current node, so that the phone expression inside the xsl:for-each element is evaluated with an order element as the current node. Effectively, it selects the phone child element of the current order element.

<xsl:if>

```
<xsl:if
  test = boolean-expression>
  <!-- Content: template -->
</xsl:if>
```

The xsl:if instruction instantiates its template content only if the XPath expression in its test attribute evaluates to true after converting it to a boolean.

For example, the following xsl:if instruction will output a comma to the result tree only if the current node is not the last node in the current node list:

```
<xsl:if test="position() != last()">
  <xsl:text>,</xsl:text>
</xsl:if>
```

<xsl:import>

```
<xsl:import
  href = uri-reference/>
```

The xsl:import element is a top-level element that imports another stylesheet into the current stylesheet. It is unique among the top-level elements; if present, it must come before all other top-level elements. In other words, all xsl:import elements in a stylesheet must occur as the first children of the xsl:stylesheet or xsl:transform element.

The value of the `href` attribute is a URI reference to the stylesheet being imported. It is resolved relative to the base URI of the `xsl:import` element itself.

Unlike `xsl:include`, `xsl:import` enables one stylesheet to override definitions in another stylesheet. If there are any like-named global variables, named templates, or multiple matching template rules, then those with the highest *import precedence* are chosen. Import precedence for a given top-level element (e.g., `xsl:template`, `xsl:variable`, or `xsl:param`) is determined by where its stylesheet occurs in the *import tree*.

The top stylesheet invoked by the XSLT processor is considered to be the root of the import tree. Each of its `xsl:import` elements represents a child of the root in the import tree. Likewise, each of the `xsl:import` elements inside the imported stylesheets represents a child of the imported stylesheet in the import tree, and so on.

For example, given a stylesheet *A.xsl* that imports *B.xsl*, *C.xsl*, and *D.xsl* (in that order), and given that *B.xsl* imports *E.xsl*, and given that *D.xsl* imports *F.xsl* and *G.xsl* (in that order), the resulting import tree could be represented like the tree shown in Figure 3.

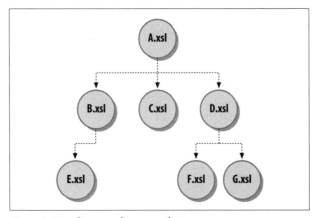

Figure 3. Visualization of an example import tree

The resulting import precedence, from highest to lowest, is: *A.xsl*, *D.xsl*, *G.xsl*, *F.xsl*, *C.xsl*, *B.xsl*, *E.xsl*. This is technically a reverse post-order traversal of the import tree. Another way of thinking about it is that there are two ordering rules. In a given stylesheet:

- All of the definitions in the current stylesheet have higher import precedence than any definitions imported by this stylesheet.
- The definitions imported later have higher import precedence than the definitions imported earlier.

If you apply these ordering rules for each stylesheet, then it will be easy to determine the relative import precedence among them.

TIP

All xsl:include directives are processed before computing the import tree. All included stylesheets are collapsed into the same "node" in the import tree so that all their definitions have the same import precedence as the stylesheet in which they're included.

<xsl:include>

```
<xsl:include
  href = uri-reference/>
```

The xsl:include element is a top-level element that includes another stylesheet into the current stylesheet. It may appear anywhere in the stylesheet as a child of the xsl:stylesheet or xsl:transform element. The included stylesheet is included at the point where the xsl:include element occurs. It behaves as if all top-level elements from the included stylesheet were copied into the including stylesheet at that point, except that any xsl:import elements in the included stylesheet are moved up to the top, after any existing xsl:import elements in the including stylesheet.

The value of the `href` attribute is a URI reference to the stylesheet being included. It is resolved relative to the base URI of the `xsl:include` element itself.

The `xsl:include` element performs inclusion at the XML tree level, which means that it makes no special provision for handling conflicts that result from the inclusion. As usual, it is an error to have duplicate global variables, duplicate named templates, and more than one matching template rule with the same priority—regardless of whether they physically occur in the same stylesheet or whether they resulted from another stylesheet being included. If you want to allow one stylesheet to override definitions in another stylesheet, use `xsl:import` instead.

<xsl:key>

```
<xsl:key
    name = qname
    match = pattern
    use = expression/>
```

The `xsl:key` element is a top-level element that is used to declare a named key index that maps a set of strings to a set of node-sets. Each `xsl:key` element defines a separate, independent set of mappings that is identified as a whole by the required `name` attribute. XSLT's key( ) function is used to retrieve the resulting node-set, given a key name and a string or set of string-values derived from a given node-set. See the key( ) function in Chapter 5.

The `xsl:key` element has the effect of building an index when the XSLT transformation begins. All nodes in the source documents that match the pattern in the required `match` attribute are included in the index.

TIP

The source documents (plural) consist of the source tree and any additional documents accessed by way of the document( ) function.

Each node that matches the pattern is subsequently mapped to a string or set of strings. This mapping is determined by evaluating the expression in the required use attribute using the matching node as the context node. If the expression returns a node-set, then the string-value of each node in the node-set is included in the set of strings that is mapped to the node. Otherwise, the expression's value is converted to a string and that one string is mapped to the node.

For example, consider this source document, which contains cross-references from order elements to part elements:

```
<partsAndOrders>
  <part sku="12345">...</part>
  <part sku="54321">...</part>
  <part sku="ABCDE">...</part>
  ...
  <order part="54321">...</order>
  <order part="ABCDE">...</order>
  ...
</partsAndOrders>
```

A stylesheet that processes this document could build a key index for efficiently following these references. The xsl:key declaration would look something like this:

```
<xsl:key name="part-by-sku" match="part" use="@sku"/>
```

Then, the key() function would be used to retrieve the part, given a particular value. For example, when the current node is an order element, the part attribute's value would be used.

```
<xsl:value-of select="key('part-by-sku',@part)/name"/>
```

TIP

The xsl:key element and the corresponding key() function provide an efficient way to traverse intra-document references that don't use actual XML ID types. See also the note about the key() function in the "Function Reference" section in Chapter 5.

<xsl:message>

```
<xsl:message
  terminate = "yes" | "no">
  <!-- Content: template -->
</xsl:message>
```

The xsl:message instruction provides a way for an XSLT stylesheet to send a message (such as a stylesheet-specific warning, error, or diagnostics message) to a target other than the result tree. Where the message gets sent is dependent on the XSLT processor, but it usually gets output to the command-line window, if applicable, or *stderr* on Unix-based systems. The content of the message is the XML fragment resulting from the template content inside the xsl:message element.

If the optional terminate attribute is set to yes, then the XSLT process is terminated when the instruction is instantiated (after the message has been sent). This is useful for so-called "fatal errors." The terminate attribute's default value is no.

For example, xsl:message can be used to help debug a stylesheet:

```
<xsl:message>
  <xsl:text>The content of the $nodes variable is:
    </xsl:text>
  <xsl:copy-of select="$nodes"/>
</xsl:message>
```

<xsl:namespace-alias>

```
<xsl:namespace-alias
  stylesheet-prefix = prefix | "#default"
  result-prefix = prefix | "#default"/>
```

The xsl:namespace-alias element is a top-level element that is useful for XSLT stylesheets that generate another XSLT stylesheet as the result. It provides a way to disambiguate between elements in the XSLT namespace that are actual instructions and elements in the XSLT namespace that are literal result elements meant to appear in the result. The required stylesheet-prefix and result-prefix attributes refer to declared namespaces in the stylesheet by their prefixes (or #default for the default namespace). The effect of the xsl:namespace-alias element is that all literal result elements in the stylesheet, that are in the namespace identified by the stylesheet-prefix attribute, will appear in the result tree in the namespace identified by the result-prefix attribute. The stylesheet-prefix namespace is thus a temporary namespace that serves as an alias for the result-prefix namespace.

Here is an example stylesheet that generates another stylesheet. Without xsl:namespace-alias, the stylesheet author would have to use xsl:element for all the result elements, so that they would not be mistaken for XSLT instructions.

```
<xsl:stylesheet version="1.0"
  xmlns:xsl="http://www.w3.org/1999/XSL/Transform"
  xmlns:out="dummy">

  <xsl:namespace-alias stylesheet-prefix="out"
    result-prefix="xsl"/>

  <xsl:template match="/">
    <out:stylesheet version="1.0">
      <out:template match="/">
        ...
      </out:template>
    </out:stylesheet>
  </xsl:template>

</xsl:stylesheet>
```

All elements in the xsl namespace are actual XSLT elements to be interpreted as such in the current process, whereas all elements in the out namespace are just literal result elements whose final namespace, after resolving the namespace alias, will be the XSLT namespace.

<xsl:number>

```
<xsl:number
  level = "single" | "multiple" | "any"
  count = pattern
  from = pattern
  value = number-expression
  format = { string }
  lang = { nmtoken }
  letter-value = { "alphabetic" | "traditional" }
  grouping-separator = { char }
  grouping-size = { number } />
```

The xsl:number instruction is used to insert a formatted number into the result tree. It performs two primary functions, both applying to positive integers:

- Assigning the current node a sequence number based on its position in the source tree
- Formatting the number

It is possible to use xsl:number purely for its formatting capabilities. You can do that by supplying the number value yourself as an expression in the value attribute. The expression value is converted to a number as if by a call to the number( ) function. It is then rounded to the nearest integer, and the result is converted to a string, according to the formatting configuration specified by xsl:number's formatting attributes (format, lang, letter-value, grouping-separator, and grouping-size), which we'll discuss shortly.

TIP

When xsl:number assigns a sequence number to the current node—i.e., when the value attribute is absent—the only context it consults is the current node. The current node list and context size (what position( ) returns) are irrelevant.

If the value attribute is absent, the number is determined based on the position of the current node in the source tree. The level, count, and from attributes configure how that number is assigned. (When the value attribute is present, the level, count, and from attributes are ignored.)

The count and from attributes both contain patterns as their values. See the "Patterns" section in Chapter 3. Generally speaking, the count pattern determines which nodes will be counted, and the from pattern determines where the counting will begin. Precisely how this works in each case depends on the value of the level attribute. In all cases, when the count attribute is absent, it defaults to a pattern that matches any node with the same node type as the current node, and, if the current node has a name (e.g., because it's an element), with the same expanded-name as the current node.

There are three general use cases, represented by the three possible values of the level attribute, as shown in Table 9.

Table 9. Three general use cases for xsl:number

Value of the level attribute	Use case and behavior
single (default)	This is for numbering a sequence of nodes at the same level, such as the items in a list.
	The sequence number in this case is the sum of 1 and the number of preceding siblings of a particular target node that match the count pattern. If the current node matches the count pattern, then it functions as the target node. Otherwise, the processor searches the ancestors of the current node for a node that matches the count pattern. The first node it finds that matches the count pattern is used as the target node. However, if the from attribute is specified, then the only ancestors that are searched are those that are descendants of the nearest ancestor that matches the from pattern. If no target node is found, then the result is empty.
	Note: The from attribute is not normally useful when level="single" is specified.

Table 9. Three general use cases for xsl:number (continued)

Value of the level attribute	Use case and behavior
`multiple`	This is for numbering hierarchical sections and subsections, such as sections in an outline—e.g., I.A.2.b.
	The sequence number in this case is a composite of multiple numbers, each of which is the sum of 1 and the number of preceding siblings of a target node for a particular level that match the `count` pattern. The list of individual sequence numbers corresponds to the list of target nodes, in document order. To find the target nodes, the processor searches the `ancestor-or-self` axis for nodes that match the `count` pattern. Each node that matches the `count` pattern is included in the list. However, if the `from` attribute is specified, then the only ancestors that are searched are those that are descendants of the nearest ancestor that matches the `from` pattern. If no target nodes are found, then the result is empty.
`any`	This is for numbering a sequence of nodes that may appear at any level of the document hierarchy, such as footnotes or comments.
	The sequence number in this case is the number of nodes in the document up to and including the current node that match the `count` pattern, excluding namespace and attribute nodes. (Technically, this set is the union of the members of the `preceding` and `ancestor-or-self` axes that match the `count` pattern.) However, if the `from` attribute is specified, then only nodes that come after the nearest node that matches the `from` pattern are considered.

As mentioned earlier, the `format`, `lang`, `letter-value`, `grouping-separator`, and `grouping-size` attributes configure how the sequence number (or list of sequence numbers when `level="multiple"`) is converted to a string.

The `format` attribute is a string that consists of an alternating sequence of *format tokens* and *separator tokens*. Format tokens consist of alphanumeric characters; separator tokens consist of non-alphanumeric characters. Each format token specifies the string to be used to represent the number 1 for the sequence number that corresponds to its position in the format string. The nth format token in the format string formats the nth sequence number in the list of numbers to be formatted. (Thus, it's useful to have more than one format token in the format string only when `level="multiple"`.) If there are more numbers than format tokens, the last format token will be used to format the remaining numbers. When the `format` attribute is absent, it defaults to the value 1 (a single format token with no separator tokens).

Separator tokens (consisting of non-alphanumeric characters) may appear at the beginning or end of the format string; in that case, the constructed string will begin or end with the corresponding token. Separator tokens that appear between format tokens serve to separate the numbers within a list of sequence numbers (i.e., when `level="multiple"`). In particular, each number after the first will be separated from the preceding number by the separator token preceding the format token used to format that number. If the `format` string contains no separator tokens, a default separator of "." (a period) is used to separate the numbers in the constructed string.

Numbering sequences can be numeric or alphabetic, depending on the value of the format token. Table 10 shows some example format tokens and the sequences they generate.

Table 10. Example format tokens and the sequences they generate

Format token	Generated sequence
1	1 2 3 4 … 10 11 12 …
A	A B C … Z AA BB CC …
a	a b c … z aa bb cc …
i	i ii iii iv v vi vii viii ix x …
I	I II III IV V VI VII VIII IX X …

The `lang` attribute indicates which language's alphabet should be used for alphabetic numbering. Its default value depends on the system environment.

The letter-value attribute is used to disambiguate between numbering sequences for languages in which two different numbering sequences use the same initial alphabetic character. A value of alphabetic indicates that the numbering should follow the alphabet. A value of traditional indicates that the other numbering sequence in that language should be used.

The grouping-separator and grouping-size attributes must occur together. If only one of the two is specified, it is ignored. The grouping-separator attribute specifies the character that should be used to separate groups (e.g., thousands) within the number, and grouping-size specifies the size of each group (normally three). For example, grouping-separator="," and grouping-size="3" would construct numbers in this format: 10,000,000.

Here is an example of the first use case, numbering the items in a list. Given a list of item elements such as this:

```
<item>apples</item>
<item>bananas</item>
<item>oranges</item>
<item>pears</item>
```

and a template rule like this:

```
<xsl:template match="item">
  <xsl:number format="1. "/>
  <xsl:apply-templates/>
</xsl:template>
```

the following result would be created:

```
1. apples
2. bananas
3. oranges
4. pears
```

Next is an example of the second use case, numbering hierarchical sections and subsections. Given a document that has this structure:

```
<doc>
  <sect1>
    <title>Dissertation on Fruit</title>
    <sect2>
      <title>Apples</title>
      <sect3>
        <title>Flavor</title>
        ...
      </sect3>
      <sect3>
        <title>Color</title>
        ...
      </sect3>
      <sect3>
        <title>Size</title>
        ...
      </sect3>
    </sect2>
    ...
  </sect1>
  ...
</doc>
```

and a template rule like this:

```
<xsl:template match="title">
  <xsl:number level="multiple"
              count="sect1 | sect2 | sect3"
              format="I.A.1 "/>
  <xsl:apply-templates/>
</xsl:template>
```

the following titles will be produced:

```
I Dissertation on Fruit
  I.A Apples
    I.A.1 Flavor
    I.A.2 Color
    I.A.3 Size
  I.B Bananas
    I.B.1 Flavor
    I.B.2 Color
    etc.
```

Finally, here is an example of the third use case: numbering a sequence of items that may appear at any level of the document hierarchy. Given a document that has note elements at different levels of the hierarchy, such as this:

```
<doc>
  <prologue>
    <note>Don't count me.</note>
  </prologue>
  <section>
    <note>This is a note.</note>
    <p>... <note>This is also a note.</note></p>
    <p>... <i><note>This is an emphasized note.</note></i>
    </p>
  </section>
  <note>This is the last note.</note>
</doc>
```

and a template rule like this:

```
<xsl:template match="section//note | doc/note">
  <xsl:number level="any" from="section[1]" format="1. "/>
  <xsl:apply-templates/>
</xsl:template>
```

then the following result will be produced:

```
Don't count me.


1. This is a note.
... 2. This is also a note.
... 3. This is an emphasized note.

4. This is the last note.
```

<xsl:otherwise>

```
<xsl:otherwise>
  <!-- Content: template -->
</xsl:otherwise>
```

The xsl:otherwise element is a special element because it may occur occur as the optional last child of the xsl:choose instruction. See "<xsl:choose>."

<xsl:output>

```
<xsl:output
  method = "xml" | "html" | "text" | qname-but-not-ncname
  version = nmtoken
  encoding = string
  omit-xml-declaration = "yes" | "no"
  standalone = "yes" | "no"
  doctype-public = string
  doctype-system = string
  cdata-section-elements = qnames
  indent = "yes" | "no"
  media-type = string />
```

The xsl:output element is a top-level element that provides
hints as to how the result tree should be serialized. They are
only hints because, depending on the processing context, the
XSLT processor may ignore them, or it may hand off serialization to a different software component altogether.

The method attribute indicates what format the serialized
result tree should be in. The built-in formats are xml, html,
and text. The XSLT processor may also provide other output methods, provided that they are identified by a QName
with a prefix. The output method affects various aspects of
serialization, such as how markup characters are serialized.
In text format, for example, markup characters (<, &, and >)
are serialized as literal characters, rather than entity references. In xml format, the result tree is serialized as a well-
formed XML document or "well-balanced" XML fragment.
In html format, the result tree is serialized in such a way that
the HTML result is rendered correctly by legacy browsers.

When the method attribute (or the entire xsl:output element)
is absent, the XSLT processor dynamically chooses between
xml and html as the default output method. If the name of the
document element of the result tree is any spelling of "HTML"
(e.g., html, HTML, htML), and if it is not in a namespace, the html
output method is used. Otherwise, the xml output method is
used.

The rest of xsl:output's attributes provide parameters for the output method that is in effect. Which parameters are applicable depends on the value of the method attribute. Table 11 shows the applicability and default value of each parameter, for each of the built-in output methods (xml, html, and text). A grayed-out field means that the parameter is not applicable to that output method.

Table 11. Default values of applicable output method parameters

Parameter name	method="xml"	method="html"	method="text"
media-type	text/xml	text/html	text/plain
encoding	UTF-8 or UTF-16	[system-dependent]	[system-dependent]
version	1.0	4.0	
indent	no	yes	
doctype-system	[none]	[none]	
doctype-public	[none]	[none]	
omit-xml-declaration	no		
standalone	[none]		
cdata-section-elements	[none]		

The version attribute indicates the version of the output method. The encoding attribute indicates what character encoding the result should be in. The omit-xml-declaration attribute specifies whether an XML declaration should be output in the result; its value must be yes or no. The standalone attribute specifies the (yes or no) value of a standalone document declaration to include in the XML declaration. When absent, no standalone declaration is output. The doctype-public and doctype-system attributes indicate which public and system identifiers, respectively, should be used in the document type declaration. The cdata-section-elements attribute specifies a list of the names of elements whose text node children should be wrapped in CDATA sections in the result. The indent attribute indicates whether additional whitespace should be added to the result to increase the document's readability; its value must be yes or no. The media-type attribute specifies the media type (MIME content type) of the result.

<xsl:param>

```
<xsl:param
  name = qname
  select = expression>
  <!-- Content: template -->
</xsl:param>
```

The xsl:param element is both a top-level element and a special element. As a top-level element, it represents a global stylesheet parameter; how its value is set is implementation-dependent. (A common technique for command-line processors is to use command-line arguments to set stylesheet parameter values.) In its special form, an xsl:param element must occur as the first child (along with any other xsl:param elements) of the xsl:template element. In that case, it specifies a template parameter whose scope is limited to the template in which it is declared. The required name attribute specifies the name of the parameter. An optional default value can be supplied using either the select attribute or the template content of the xsl:param element. If the select attribute is absent and the xsl:param element is empty, then the default value of the parameter is an empty string. The parameter is initialized to the default value only when no parameter is explicitly passed to the template or stylesheet.

The xsl:param element serves the same function as the xsl:variable element, except that its default value is optional and can be overridden by a parameter passed to the stylesheet or template. See "<xsl:variable>."

<xsl:preserve-space>

```
<xsl:preserve-space
  elements = tokens />
```

The xsl:preserve-space element is a top-level element that specifies a list of names of elements whose whitespace-only text node children should *not* be stripped from the source document prior to the transformation. Its use is only necessary when xsl:strip-space is also used in the same stylesheet because the default behavior is to not strip any text nodes from the source document. Its purpose is to provide a list of exceptions to the list specified by xsl:strip-space. For a fuller explanation of this process, see "<xsl:strip-space>."

<xsl:processing-instruction>

```
<xsl:processing-instruction
  name = { ncname }>
  <!-- Content: template -->
</xsl:processing-instruction>
```

The xsl:processing-instruction instruction is used to insert a processing instruction (PI) node into the result tree. Its required name attribute specifies the PI target. Its content is a template for the string-value of the processing instruction. The resulting value must not include the string "?>".

For example, the following instruction creates an XML stylesheet PI in the result:

```
<xsl:processing-instruction name="xml-stylesheet">
  <xsl:text>type="text/xsl" href="style.xsl"</xsl:text>
</xsl:processing-instruction>
```

The resulting PI looks like this:

```
<?xml-stylesheet type="text/xsl" href="style.xsl"?>
```

<xsl:sort>

```
<xsl:sort
  select = string-expression
```

```
lang = { nmtoken }
data-type = { "text" | "number" | qname-but-not-ncname }
order = { "ascending" | "descending" }
case-order = { "upper-first" | "lower-first" } />
```

The xsl:sort element is a special element that may occur
only as a child of xsl:apply-templates or as the first child
(along with any other xsl:sort elements) of xsl:for-each. It
causes these instructions to process the relevant node-set in a
different order than the default order, which is document
order. Each xsl:sort element that is present specifies a sort
key. The first xsl:sort element specifies the primary sort key,
the second specifies the secondary sort key, etc.

The select attribute contains an expression that is evaluated
for each node in the node-set, using that node as the current
node and the entire node-set in document order as the current node list. The result is converted to a string, and that
string is used as the sort key for that node. The select
attribute's default value is the expression ".", which effectively causes the string-value of the node itself to be used as
the sort key.

The rest of xsl:sort's attributes configure how the sort keys
are sorted. Each of these is interpreted as an attribute value
template (AVT), evaluated relative to the current node *outside* the containing xsl:for-each or xsl:apply-templates
instruction. Table 12 shows the four parameters, their
allowed values, and their default values.

Table 12. Sort key configuration parameters

Parameter name	Allowed values	Default value
order	ascending descending	ascending
lang	en, en-US, fr, etc.	[system-dependent]
data-type	text number [any QName with prefix]	text
case-order	upper-first lower-first	[language-dependent]

The order attribute specifies whether the sort keys should be sorted in ascending or descending order. The lang attribute specifies the language of the sort keys. The system environment determines its default value.

The data-type attribute specifies the data type of the sort keys. A value of text causes the strings to be sorted lexicographically (e.g., in alphabetical order) as appropriate for the language (e.g., English). A value of number causes the sort keys to be converted to numbers and sorted numerically. Other implementation-defined data types can be referenced using a namespace-qualified QName. Finally, the case-order attribute specifies whether upper- or lowercase characters should be sorted first (when data-type="text").

The following example sorts the product elements alphabetically by the value of their title children:

```
<xsl:for-each select="product">
  <xsl:sort select="title"/>
  ...
</xsl:for-each>
```

<xsl:strip-space>

```
<xsl:strip-space
  elements = tokens />
```

The xsl:strip-space element is a top-level element that specifies which elements in the source tree should have their whitespace-only text node children stripped from them before beginning the transformation. The value of the required elements attribute is a list of patterns, each of which must conform to the XPath 1.0 NameTest production:

```
[37] NameTest      '*'
                 | NCName ':' '*'
                 | Qname
```

TIP

This is excerpted from the full XPath 1.0 grammar, which is included in Appendix A.

In other words, the list must only contain patterns such as `*`, `xyz:*`, `foo`, `xyz:foo`.

Whitespace stripping is an optional pre-process that can be applied to the source tree. Whitespace-only text nodes are text nodes whose string-value consists of space, tab, carriage return, or line feed characters only (#x20, #x9, #xD, or #xA). A text node that has at least one non-whitespace character is never stripped. By default, no text nodes are stripped from the source tree. However, if the `xsl:strip-space` element is present, all elements in the source tree that match one of the patterns in the `elements` attribute have all of their whitespace-only text node children stripped from them before the transformation begins.

There are two exceptions to this rule. If an individual element in the source tree has an ancestor element with `xml:space="preserve"` and no closer element has `xml:space="default"`, then that element's whitespace-only text node children are preserved, regardless of whether the element matches a pattern in the `elements` list. The other exception is when the element matches one of the patterns in the `xsl:preserve-space` element's list of elements to preserve. The `xsl:preserve-space` element also has a required `elements` attribute that contains a list of patterns matching the XPath NameTest production. Its purpose is to specify exceptions to `xsl:strip-space`'s list of elements from which to strip whitespace. See also "<xsl:preserve-space>."

Conflicts between matches in `xsl:strip-space` and `xsl:preserve-space` are resolved in the same way as conflicts between template rules. First, any match with lower import precedence than another is ignored. For example, if the same node matches two patterns (in `xsl:strip-space` or `xsl:preserve-space`'s `elements` list), one in an importing stylesheet and one in an imported stylesheet, then the pattern in the imported stylesheet is ignored. Second, any matching patterns that have a lower default priority than the default priority of another match are ignored.

The following example shows a typical use of the xsl:strip-space and xsl:preserve-space elements:

```
<xsl:stylesheet version="1.0"
  xmlns:xsl="http://www.w3.org/1999/XSL/Transform">

  <xsl:strip-space elements="*"/>
  <xsl:preserve-space elements="pre"/>

  ...

</xsl:stylesheet>
```

In this example, all elements in the source tree except for pre elements have their whitespace-only text node children stripped from them. (The pre pattern overrides the * pattern because it has higher priority.)

<xsl:stylesheet>

```
<xsl:stylesheet
  id = id
  extension-element-prefixes = tokens
  exclude-result-prefixes = tokens
  version = number>
  <!-- Content: (xsl:import*, top-level-elements) -->
</xsl:stylesheet>
```

The xsl:stylesheet element is the root, or document, element of the stylesheet. It is interchangeable with xsl:transform. The version attribute is required and indicates the version of XSLT being used, e.g., 1.0. The id attribute is only useful when the entire XSLT stylesheet is embedded inside another XML document.

The extension-element-prefixes and exclude-result-prefixes attributes both contain a list of namespace prefix tokens corresponding to namespaces that are declared in the stylesheet.

It is easy to end up with undesired namespace declarations in the result tree. That's because, by default, a literal result element in the stylesheet automatically creates an element copy in the result tree that includes copies of all of its namespace nodes. Use the `exclude-result-prefixes` attribute to list all the namespaces that should *not* be included in the result tree at the end of the transformation.

The `extension-element-prefixes` attribute indicates which namespaces are namespaces of extension elements used in the stylesheet so that the XSLT processor will know to treat elements in one of these namespaces as an extension element. In addition, the namespaces listed in the `extension-element-prefixes` attribute are included in the list of namespaces to exclude from being copied to the result tree. See also the "Extension Elements" section in Chapter 6.

The allowed child elements of the `xsl:stylesheet` element are listed in the "Top-Level Elements" section earlier in this chapter.

\<xsl:template>

```
<xsl:template
  match = pattern
  name = qname
  priority = number
  mode = qname>
  <!-- Content: (xsl:param*, template) -->
</xsl:template>
```

The `xsl:template` element is a top-level element that is used to define *named templates* and/or *template rules*. A named template is an `xsl:template` element that has a `name` attribute. It is invoked via the `xsl:call-template` instruction. A template rule is an `xsl:template` element that has a `match` attribute. It is invoked explicitly via the `xsl:apply-templates` instruction and implicitly by XSLT's built-in template rules. A single `xsl:template` element functions both as a named template and as a template rule, if both the `name` and `match` attributes are present. All `xsl:template` elements must at least have either a `name` attribute or a `match` attribute.

The value of the `match` attribute is an XSLT pattern. It is an error if the pattern contains a variable reference. See the "Patterns" section in Chapter 3.

The optional `mode` and `priority` attributes are only allowed on template rules, i.e., when the `match` attribute is also present. The `mode` attribute indicates what mode this template rule is in. Modes are a way of segmenting template rules into different scopes. They are useful when you need to apply different template rules to the same node. A template rule in a given mode can be invoked only by an `xsl:apply-templates` instruction whose `mode` attribute has the same value, or by a built-in template rule in the same mode. When the `mode` attribute is absent, the template rule is in the single unnamed mode and can be invoked only by an `xsl:apply-templates` instruction that does not have a `mode` attribute, or by a built-in template rule in the unnamed mode.

The optional `priority` attribute allows you to override the *default priority* for a particular template rule. (The default priority is determined by the syntax of the pattern in the `match` attribute; see the "Priority" section in Chapter 3.)

Named templates and template rules can have named parameters, which are declared using one or more `xsl:param` elements that must occur as the first children of the element. Parameters are initialized by the `xsl:call-template` or `xsl:apply-templates` instruction used to instantiate the template. See "<xsl:param>."

For a complete discussion of the XSLT processing model, including what the built-in template rules are, how templates rules are selected, and how template rule priority is determined, see the "Processing Model" section in Chapter 3.

<xsl:text>

```
<xsl:text
  disable-output-escaping = "yes" | "no">
  <!-- Content: #PCDATA -->
</xsl:text>
```

The xsl:text instruction is used to insert a text node into the result tree. While text nodes can also be inserted in any template context without using an xsl:text element, it can be useful for maintaining consistent code formatting (indentation) in an XSLT stylesheet, while being able to precisely control what whitespace should appear in the result tree. It's also useful if you want to insert a whitespace-only text node into the result tree. That's because XSLT processors strip all whitespace-only text nodes from your stylesheet when it builds the stylesheet tree—except for those inside the xsl:text element (or declared with xml:space="preserve").

For example, the following template rule does not use an xsl:text element. It outputs exactly one text node whose value is *<name>* is my name.

```
<xsl:template name="my-name">
  <xsl:value-of select="name"/> is my name.</xsl:template>
```

To achieve the same effect while still being able to maintain consistent element indentation, you can use the xsl:text element like so:

```
<xsl:template name="my-name">
  <xsl:value-of select="name"/>
  <xsl:text> is my name.</xsl:text>
</xsl:template>
```

For an explanation of the disable-output-escaping attribute, see "Disabling Output Escaping" in Chapter 3.

<xsl:transform>

```
<xsl:transform
  id = id
  extension-element-prefixes = tokens
  exclude-result-prefixes = tokens
  version = number>
  <!-- Content: (xsl:import*, top-level-elements) -->
</xsl:stylesheet>
```

The xsl:transform element is interchangeable with xsl:
stylesheet as the root, or document, element of an XSLT
stylesheet. It behaves exactly the same as xsl:stylesheet.
Which element name you use is a matter of personal preference. See "<xsl:stylesheet>."

<xsl:value-of>

```
<xsl:value-of
  select = string-expression
  disable-output-escaping = "yes" | "no" />
```

The xsl:value-of instruction creates a text node in the result
tree. The required select attribute is evaluated, the result is
converted to a string, and the resulting string is used as the
string-value of the text node.

TIP

When the select expression returns a node-set containing more than one node, the string-value of only the first
node of the node-set in document order is used, and the
rest are ignored. This is according to the rule for converting a node-set to a string, described in the "Data Type
Conversions" section in Chapter 5.

For an explanation of the disable-output-escaping attribute,
see the "Disabling Output Escaping" section in Chapter 3.

Here is an example use of the xsl:value-of instruction:

```
<xsl:value-of select="/page/title"/>
```

This creates a text node in the result tree whose string-value
is the string-value of the title element in the source tree. If
there is more than one title element, only the first title element in document order is used.

<xsl:variable>

```
<xsl:variable
  name = qname
  select = expression>
  <!-- Content: template -->
</xsl:variable>
```

The xsl:variable element is both an instruction and a top-level element. As a top-level element, it represents a global variable. As an instruction, it represents a local variable whose scope is limited to the element in which it is defined. The required name attribute specifies the name of the variable. The variable's value is specified using either the select attribute or the template content. See also "<xsl:param>."

If the select attribute is present, then the element must be empty. If the select attribute is absent and the xsl:variable element has non-empty content, then the value of the variable is a result tree fragment whose content is specified using the template content of the xsl:variable element. If the select attribute is absent and the xsl:variable element is empty, then the value of the variable is an empty string. See the "Result Tree Fragments" section in Chapter 2.

<xsl:when>

```
<xsl:when
  test = boolean-expression>
  <!-- Content: template -->
</xsl:when>
```

The xsl:when element is a special element that may only occur as a child of xsl:choose. See "<xsl:choose>."

<xsl:with-param>

```
<xsl:with-param
  name = qname
  select = expression>
  <!-- Content: template -->
</xsl:with-param>
```

The xsl:with-param element is a special element that must occur as a child of xsl:apply-templates or xsl:call-template. It passes a named parameter to the template rule or named template that is invoked. The value is specified the same way as with xsl:variable and xsl:param; i.e., you can use either the select attribute or the template content (which passes a result tree fragment) to specify the value of the parameter. If the select attribute is absent and the xsl:with-param element is empty, then the value passed is an empty string. If you pass a parameter to a template in which the parameter is not declared, it is simply ignored.

Here is an example of a parameter being passed to a named template:

```
<xsl:call-template name="show-price">
  <xsl:with-param name="price" select="35"/>
</xsl:call-template>
```

And here is a corresponding named template:

```
<xsl:template name="show-price">
  <xsl:param name="price"/>
  ...
</xsl:template>
```

See also "<xsl:apply-templates>" and "<xsl:call-template>."

CHAPTER 5

Functions

This chapter contains an alphabetical reference of the 36 functions contained in the XPath and XSLT languages. The majority of these come from XPath.

XPath Functions

The XPath recommendation itself groups its 27 functions into four categories, according to their role, as shown in Table 13.

Table 13. XPath functions

Node-set functions	String functions	Boolean functions	Number functions
last( )	string( )	boolean( )	number( )
position( )	concat( )	not( )	sum( )
count( )	starts-with( )	true( )	floor( )
id( )	contains( )	false( )	ceiling( )
local-name( )	substring-before( )	lang( )	round( )
namespace-uri( )	substring-after( )		
name( )	substring( )		
	string-length( )		
	normalize-space( )		
	translate( )		

The only function in XPath 1.0 that returns a node-set is the
id( ) function. The rest return a number, string, or boolean.

XSLT Functions

XSLT adds nine functions of its own:

```
document( )                generate-id( )
key( )                     system-property( )
format-number( )           element-available( )
current( )                 function-available( )
unparsed-entity-uri( )
```

Of these, three return a node-set: document( ), key( ), and
current( ). The other functions return a number, string, or
boolean.

Data Type Conversions

XSLT and XPath are dynamically typed languages. Whenever it is possible for the XSLT processor to convert a given
value to a value of the expected data type, it does so automatically. The particular rules for converting to each of the
four XPath data types are described next.

TIP

When being converted to another data type, result tree
fragments behave exactly the same as a node-set containing a single root node.

Strings

Whenever a string value is expected, the given value is converted to a string according to these rules:

- A node-set converts to the string-value of the node in the node-set that is first in document order.
- Boolean false converts to the string `false`, and boolean true converts to the string `true`.
- A number converts to a string according to these rules:

    —NaN ("Not a Number") converts to the string `NaN`.

    —Both positive zero and negative zero convert to the string `0`.

    —Positive infinity converts to the string `Infinity`.

    —Negative infinity converts to the string `-Infinity`.

    —Integers are represented with no decimal point and no leading zeros.

    —Nonintegers include at least one digit before and after the decimal point, with no superfluous zeros beyond the required digits.

    —Negative numbers are preceded by a minus sign (-).

An automatic string conversion takes place whenever a non-string value appears as any of these:

- A function argument that is expected to be a string, e.g., `string-length(100)`
- The value returned by the select expression of the `xsl:value-of` instruction, e.g., `<xsl:value-of select="/foo/bar"/>`
- A number or boolean returned by the select expression of the `xsl:copy-of` instruction, e.g., `<xsl:copy-of select=".39"/>`

Automatic string conversion also takes place as an intermediate step when converting a node-set to a number. Finally, you can also use the `string( )` function to explicitly convert a value to a string.

Numbers

Whenever a number is expected, the given value is converted to a number according to these rules:

- A string converts to a number according to the IEEE 754 round-to-the-nearest rule, after stripping any leading and trailing whitespace; any string that does not represent a valid number converts to NaN ("Not a Number").

- A node-set first converts to a string according to the XPath string conversion rules (as if by a call to the string( ) function) and then converts to a number in the same way as a string.

- Boolean true converts to 1; boolean false converts to 0.

An automatic conversion to number occurs whenever a non-number value appears as any of these:

- A function argument that is expected to be a number, e.g., round(foo)

- An operand to an arithmetic expression, e.g., foo * 3

- A string being compared to a number, e.g., substring(foo,1,1) = 3

- Each node's string-value when comparing a node-set to a number, e.g., foo = 3

Booleans

Whenever a boolean is expected, the given value is converted to a boolean according to these rules:

- A string converts to false if the string is empty, true otherwise.

- A node-set converts to false if the node-set is empty, true otherwise.

- A number converts to false if the number is 0 or NaN, true otherwise.

An automatic conversion to boolean occurs whenever a non-boolean value appears as any of these:

- A function argument that is expected to be a boolean, e.g., not(bar)
- A non-numeric value of a predicate expression, e.g., bar in foo[bar]
- An operand to an and or or expression, e.g., foo and bar
- A value being compared to a boolean, e.g., foo=true( ) and number(foo)=true( )

You can also use the boolean( ) function to explicitly convert a value to a boolean.

Node-Sets

No other types can be converted to a node-set. For example, if you pass a string to a function where a node-set is expected, you will get an error. When a node-set argument is expected, you must pass only a node-set. (Similarly, you cannot convert a value to a result tree fragment; result tree fragments can only be created using an xsl:variable instruction.)

Function Reference

This reference section contains all 36 of the functions that are built into XPath and XSLT. Each of the nine XSLT-specific functions is identified as such at the end of its function description.

Function signatures use the following format, where a question mark (?) indicates an optional argument:

> *return-type* function-name(*argument-type, argument-type?*)

An argument placeholder's name denotes the expected data type of the argument. When a value of any other data type is passed to the function, it is automatically converted to the expected type insofar as this is possible according to the rules defined in the "Data Type Conversions" section, earlier in this chapter.

When the argument placeholder's name is *object*, the function behaves differently depending on the data type of the argument you pass to it, rather than uniformly converting all types to a single expected type. The only functions that have *object* as an argument are the document( ), id( ), and key( ) functions.

boolean boolean(*boolean*)

> This function returns the value of its argument after converting it to a boolean, according to the rules for converting non-boolean values to booleans. If the argument is omitted, it defaults to a node-set containing the context node as its only member.

> For example, boolean('a string') returns true because the string is nonempty.

> For the precise conversion rules, see the "Booleans" section earlier in this chapter.

number ceiling(*number*)

>   This function rounds up the argument to the nearest whole number. For example, ceiling(5.2) returns the number 6.
>
>   See also the floor( ) function.

string concat(*string, string, string**)

>   This function returns the concatenation of its string arguments. It is the only XSLT/XPath function that allows a variable number of arguments. For example, concat("Hello ","to the"," world") returns the string Hello to the world.

boolean contains(*string, string*)

>   This function returns true if the second argument is a substring of the first argument, and false otherwise. For example, contains('Hello','ell') returns true.

number count(*node-set*)

>   This function returns the number of nodes in the argument node-set.

node-set current( )

>   This function returns a node-set containing the *current node*. The current node is the context node in effect at the topmost level of a given XPath expression, as distinct from the context node in effect within a given subexpression.
>
>   Though the expressions . and current( ) refer to the same node when they occur as complete expressions, they refer to different nodes when inside an XPath predicate expression. For example, the expression /foo/bar[.=current( )] selects all /foo/bar elements whose string-value is equal to the string-value of the context node in effect at the outermost level of the expression, i.e., the current node. Unless you first store the current node in a variable, the current( ) function is the only way to access the current node from within a predicate expression like the one in the example.
>
>   (This function is specific to XSLT.)

node-set document(*object, node-set?*)

This function is used to access XML documents other than the source tree. It returns a node-set that is either empty or that contains one or more root nodes. If the first argument is a scalar (string, boolean, or number), it's converted to a string and used as the URI from which to retrieve the document. If the first argument is a node-set, then for each node in the node-set, the string-value is used as a URI to resolve. This means that if the first argument node-set contains more than one node, the function may return more than one input document (root nodes).

If the second (optional) argument node-set is supplied, then the base URI of the first node in document order is used as the base URI when retrieving documents via a relative URI (supplied by the first argument).

When the second argument is absent, the base URI depends on the type of the first argument. If the first argument is a scalar (and the second argument is absent), the base URI of the XSLT instruction in which the document( ) call appears is used as the base URI for resolving relative URIs. If the first argument is a node-set (and the second argument is absent), the base URI is the base URI of the node itself, for each node in the node-set.

Another way to state the previous definition is to break the function signature down into three separate signatures, each of which behaves differently with respect to base URI initialization:

document(*object, node-set*)

The base URI is the base URI of the first node in document order of the second argument.

document(*node-set*)

The base URI is the base URI of the node itself, for each node in the argument node-set.

document(*string*)
> The base URI is the base URI of the XSLT instruction in which the function call appears.

In the event of a retrieval error, the XSLT processor may report the error or fall back by returning an empty node-set.

For example, document('config.xml') retrieves a file named *config.xml* in the same directory as the XSLT stylesheet.

(This function is specific to XSLT.)

boolean element-available(*string*)
> This function returns true if the QName argument resolves to the name of an XSLT instruction or an extension element for which the processor has an implementation. The QName argument is expanded using the namespaces in scope for the expression. If there is no implementation available, then it will return false.

TIP

If the QName's namespace URI is null, then the function will return false because all XSLT instruction and extension element names must be namespace-qualified.

See also the function-available( ) function.

(This function is specific to XSLT.)

boolean false( )
> This function returns the boolean value false.

number floor(*number*)
> This function rounds down the argument to the nearest whole number. For example, floor(5.7) returns the number 5.

See also the ceiling( ) function.

string format-number(*number, string, string?*)

This function returns a string consisting of a formatted representation of the number in the first argument. The second argument is a format pattern string, and the third (optional) argument refers to the name of a decimal format declaration (using the xsl:decimal-format element) in the stylesheet. If the third argument is omitted, then the default decimal format will be used.

For example, format-number(43.1, '$##0.00') returns the string $43.10.

See xsl:decimal-format in Chapter 4 for a complete definition of how the format-number( ) function is evaluated.

(This function is specific to XSLT.)

boolean function-available(*string*)

This function returns true if the QName argument resolves to the name of a function in the function library. The QName argument is expanded using the namespaces in scope for the expression. If there is no implementation available, it will return false.

For example, function-available('exsl:node-set') will return true only if the current XSLT processor supports EXSLT's exsl:node-set( ) extension function (assuming that the exsl prefix maps to the namespace http://exslt.org/common). See the "EXSLT—Common" section in Chapter 6.

TIP

If the QName's namespace URI is null, then the name must match one of the built-in XSLT/XPath functions. Otherwise, it must match the name of an available extension function because all extension function names must be namespace-qualified.

See also the element-available( ) function.

(This function is specific to XSLT.)

---

string generate-id(*node-set?*)

> This function returns an automatically generated unique string identifier for the first node in document order of the argument node-set. The function is guaranteed to return a unique identifier among all nodes that are processed within a single XSLT transformation. Also, it will always generate the same identifier for the same node within a single XSLT transformation.
>
> If the node-set is empty, then the empty string is returned. If the argument is omitted, then it defaults to the context node.
>
> (This function is specific to XSLT.)

node-set id(*object*)

> This function returns a node-set containing zero or more element nodes from the same document as the context node, retrieving them by their ID value (as declared in the DTD). If the argument is a node-set, then the result is the union of the result of applying id( ) to the string-value of each of the nodes in the argument node-set. If the argument is of any other type (string, number, or boolean), then it is converted to a string and split into a whitespace-separated list of tokens. The result is a node-set containing the elements in the same document as the context node that have a unique ID equal to any of the tokens in the list.
>
> For example, id('foo bar') returns the element with unique ID foo and the element with unique ID bar.
>
> The following example illustrates the use of a node-set argument. Here is an excerpt from the XML source tree:

```
<!DOCTYPE genealogy [
<!ATTLIST person
          id ID #IMPLIED>
]>
<genealogy>
  <person parents="ABCD ASDF"/>
  <person parents="xyz"/>
```

```
<person id="ABCD">...</person>
<person id="xyz">...</person>
<person id="ASDF">...</person>
<!-- ... -->
</genealogy>
```

Given this snippet, id(//person/@parents) will return three elements, namely the person elements in the same document that have the unique IDs ABCD, ASDF, and xyz.

TIP

The id() and generate-id() functions are unrelated. Whereas the generate-id() function deals with unique identifiers that the XSLT processor automatically generates, the id() function deals with elements that are declared as having an attribute of type ID in the source document's DTD.

---

node-set key(*string, object*)

This function returns a node-set containing zero or more nodes from the same document as the context node that are keyed by a particular value. The first argument is a QName that refers to a named key index declared by the xsl:key element. The second argument provides one or more key values. If the second argument is a scalar (string, number, or boolean), then the key value is the second argument after converting it to a string. If the second argument is a node-set, then the result is the union of the result of applying the key() function to each of the nodes in the argument node-set.

For example, key('related','botany') returns all the nodes that are keyed to the string botany, as declared by the key index named related (declared using the xsl:key instruction).

See "<xsl:key>" in Chapter 4 for the definition of how a key index is created.

(This function is specific to XSLT.)

boolean lang(*string*)

This function returns true if the language of the context
node (as declared by an xml:lang attribute on it or its
nearest ancestor that has an xml:lang attribute) is the
same as or is a sublanguage of the language specified by
the argument string. Otherwise, it returns false. For
example, lang("en") would return true when the context
node is <foo xml:lang="en"/>, <foo xml:lang="en-US"/>,
etc.

number last( )

This function returns the context size.

For example, when iterating over a node-set that contains three nodes, the last( ) function will return the
number 3. That's because, in XSLT, the context size is
always set to the size of the current node list.

See the "Expression Context" section in Chapter 2.

string local-name(*node-set?*)

This function returns the local part of the expanded-
name of the first node in document order of the node-set
argument. If the argument is absent, then it defaults to
the context node.

See Chapter 1.

string name(*node-set?*)

> This function returns a QName representing the expanded-name of the first node in document order of the node-set argument. If the argument is absent, then it defaults to the context node. (Example QNames are foo, my:foo, xyz:bar, etc.)

> The QName represents the expanded-name with respect to the particular namespace declarations in scope for the node in the source document. This is usually the QName that occurred in the XML source (but could be different if there is more than one namespace declaration in scope for the same namespace URI).

> See Chapter 1.

WARNING

The name( ) function returns a QName whose namespace URI can only be resolved correctly within the namespace context of the source document, *not the stylesheet*. To reliably get the local part and the namespace URI of an element or attribute node, instead use the local-name( ) and namespace-uri( ) functions, respectively.

---

string namespace-uri(*node-set?*)

> This function returns the namespace URI of the expanded-name of the first node in document order of the argument node-set. If the argument is absent, then it defaults to the context node.

> See Chapter 1.

string normalize-space(*string?*)

> This function returns the argument string after stripping off all leading and trailing whitespace characters and converting other sequences of whitespace characters into a single space character. If the argument is omitted, then it defaults to the string-value of the context node.

The whitespace characters are space (#x20), tab (#x9), new line (#xA), and carriage return (#xD).

For example, normalize-space(" foo bar ") returns this string: foo bar.

boolean not(*boolean*)

This function returns true if the argument is false, and false otherwise. For example, not(foo) returns true if there are no child foo elements.

number number(*number?*)

This function returns the value of its argument after converting it to a number, according to the rules for converting non-number values to numbers. If the argument is omitted, then it defaults to a node-set containing the context node as its only member.

For the precise conversion rules, see the "Numbers" section earlier in this chapter.

number position( )

This function returns the context position.

For example, when iterating over the second node in the current node list, position( ) returns the number 2.

See the "Expression Context" section in Chapter 2.

number round(*number*)

This function rounds the argument to the nearest whole number, rounding up in case of a tie. For example, round(3.5) returns the number 4, but round(3.49) returns the number 3.

boolean starts-with(*string, string*)

This function returns true if the first argument string starts with the second argument string, and false otherwise. For example, starts-with('Hello','Hell') returns true.

string string(*string?*)

This function returns the value of its argument after converting it to a string, according to the rules for converting nonstring values to strings. If the argument is
omitted, then it defaults to a node-set containing the
context node as its only member.

For example, string(.5) returns the string 0.5.

For the precise conversion rules, see the "Strings" section earlier in this chapter.

number string-length(*string?*)

This function returns the length in characters of the argument string. If the argument is omitted, then it defaults
to the string-value of the context node.

For example, string-length('Hello world') returns the
number 11.

string substring(*string, number, number?*)

This function returns a substring of the first argument
string, beginning at the (1-based) index specified by the
second argument and consisting of as many characters as
specified by the third argument. If the third argument is
omitted or if it exceeds the number of characters remaining in the string, then the substring continues to the end
of the string.

For example, substring('Hello world',7) returns "world".

string substring-after(*string, string*)

This function returns the substring of the first argument that follows the first instance of the second argument string. If the second argument is not contained within the first, then the function returns the empty string.

For example, substring-after('Hello world','Hello ') returns "world".

string substring-before(*string, string*)

This function returns the substring of the first argument that precedes the first instance of the second argument string. If the second argument is not contained within the first, then the function returns the empty string.

For example, substring-before('Hello world',' world') returns "Hello".

number sum(*node-set*)

This function returns the sum of all numbers in the supplied node-set. The node-set is converted to a set of numbers by converting the string-value of each node to a number. For example, sum(//price) returns the sum of all prices, after converting the string-value of each price element to a number.

object system-property(*string*)

This function returns the value of the system property with the given name. The string argument must be a valid QName. It is expanded using the namespace declarations in scope for the expression. If there is no such system property, the function returns the empty string.

What system properties are available is dependent on the particular XSLT processor and its processing context. However, there are a minimum of three properties that all XSLT processors must initialize:

xsl:version

A number specifying the current version of XSLT. For XSLT 1.0, this is the number 1.

`xsl:vendor`
> A string identifying the vendor of the XSLT processor.

`xsl:vendor-url`
> A string URL that points to the XSLT processor vendor's web site.

(This function is specific to XSLT.)

string translate(*string*, *string*, *string*)
> This function returns a string that consists of the first argument string after replacing certain characters in that string with other characters according to a translation mapping specified by the last two argument strings. The second and third argument strings are interpreted as ordered lists of characters. Each character in the second string will be replaced by the character at the same position in the third argument string. For example, translate('Hello World', 'HW', 'hw') returns the string hello world, whereas translate('Hello World', 'HW', 'wh') returns the string wello horld.

> If the second argument string is longer than the third argument string, then the characters in the second argument that have no corresponding character in the third argument are removed from the first argument. For example, translate('Hello World', 'H w', 'h') returns the string helloorld. H is replaced by h, and the space and w characters are replaced by nothing; i.e., they are removed.

TIP

The most common use case for the translate( ) function is to convert uppercase characters to lowercase, or vice versa, by listing the entire alphabet in order, both in upper- and lowercase, like this: translate($string, 'ABCDEFGHIJKLMNOPQRSTUVWXYZ', 'abcdefghijklmnopqrstuvwxyz').

---

boolean true( )

This function returns the boolean value true.

string unparsed-entity-uri(*string*)

This function returns the URI of the unparsed entity with the specified name in the same document as the context node. If there is no such entity, it returns the empty string.

(This function is specific to XSLT.)

CHAPTER 6

Extending XSLT

XSLT 1.0 can be extended in two ways: *extension functions* and *extension elements*. The EXSLT community project (*http://www.exslt.org*) defines a number of useful extensions supported by multiple XSLT processors. This chapter contains a complete reference for the EXSLT extensions, including what processors support them. You'll also find Tip sections that compare individual EXSLT functions with new features in XSLT 2.0 and XPath 2.0.

Extension Functions

Extension functions are functions included in an XSLT processor that are not among XSLT 1.0's built-in set of functions. Unlike built-in functions, they must be namespace-qualified. When a function name includes a namespace prefix (e.g., exslt:node-set( )), an XSLT processor interprets it as a call to an extension function.

To test if a particular extension function is available in the current XSLT processor, use the function-available( ) function.

XSLT 1.0 does not include a built-in mechanism for user-defined functions (unlike XSLT 2.0), but some XSLT processors support EXSLT's func:function element, which allows users to define their own functions in XSLT. See the section "EXSLT—Functions" later in this chapter.

How to Use an Extension Function

Here is an example use of an extension function. This will work in any XSLT processor that supports the EXSLT Dates and Times module:

```
<xsl:stylesheet version="1.0"
  xmlns:xsl="http://www.w3.org/1999/XSL/Transform"
  xmlns:date="http://exslt.org/dates-and-times"
  exclude-result-prefixes="date">

  <xsl:template match="/">
    <p>Today's date is <xsl:value-of select=
        "date:date( )"/>.</p>
  </xsl:template>

</xsl:stylesheet>
```

Extension Elements

Extension elements are elements in a namespace that has been designated as an extension element namespace. Such elements are interpreted as instructions rather than literal result elements. The extension element namespaces for a stylesheet are listed in the `extension-element-prefixes` attribute on the xsl:stylesheet (or xsl:transform) root element. They can also be listed in the xsl:extension-element-prefixes attribute, which may occur on any literal result element or extension element. In that case, they are in effect for that element and its descendants. Namespace nodes for extension namespaces are automatically excluded from being copied with literal result elements to the result tree (as with the namespaces listed in the `exclude-result-prefixes` attribute).

To test if a particular extension element is available in the current XSLT processor, use the element-available( ) function.

How to Use an Extension Element

Here is an example use of an extension element. In a processor that supports the exsl:document element (an optional element in the EXSLT Common module), this stylesheet will have the effect of creating and writing to a file called *outputFile.txt*:

```
<xsl:stylesheet version="1.0"
  xmlns:xsl="http://www.w3.org/1999/XSL/Transform"
  xmlns:exsl="http://exslt.org/common"
  extension-element-prefixes="exsl">

  <xsl:template match="/">
    <exsl:document href="outputFile.txt">
      <xsl:text>Write this text to outputFile.txt.
        </xsl:text>
    </exsl:document>
    <!-- ... -->
  </xsl:template>

</xsl:stylesheet>
```

EXSLT

EXSLT (*http://www.exslt.org*) began as a collaborative project among XSLT users hoping to make their stylesheets more portable. At the time, various XSLT processors supported similar but non-portable extensions, such as an extension function for converting result tree fragments to node-sets (xalan:nodeset( ), saxon:node-set( ), etc.). Today—thanks to the EXSLT project—Xalan, Saxon, 4XSLT, and libxslt all support, for example, the exsl:node-set( ) function. You can now use that extension in all of these processors without having to make any changes to your stylesheet.

EXSLT is divided into nine modules, each of which has its own namespace for extension function and element names. Each module can define *core* and *optional* extension functions and elements. Table 14 shows the distribution of extensions into these four categories among EXSLT's nine modules.

Table 14. Make-up of the EXSLT modules

Module	Functions		Elements	
	Core	Optional	Core	Optional
Common	2			1
Dates and Times	18	9		1
Functions			2	1
Math	4	14		
Random	1			
Sets	6			
Dynamic		6		
Regular Expressions		3		
Strings		8		

In order for an XSLT processor to rightfully claim support for a particular module, it must implement all of the core extensions in that module.

This chapter features four XSLT processors and one third-party library (EXSLT.NET, which adds EXSLT support to Microsoft's XSLT processor in the .NET Framework). All are open source and available for download:

4XSLT
http://www.4suite.org

libxslt
http://www.xmlsoft.org

Xalan-J
http://xml.apache.org/xalan-j

Saxon
http://saxon.sf.net

EXSLT.NET
http://workspaces.gotdotnet.com/exslt (see also *nxslt.exe*, the ".NET XSLT Command Line Utility," which includes the

EXSLT.NET implementation: *http://www.tkachenko.com/dotnet/nxslt.html*)

Table 15 lists the level of support that each of these processors has for each EXSLT module.

Table 15. Processors' support for EXSLT modules

Module	4XSLT	libxslt	Xalan-J	Saxon[a]	EXSLT.NET
Common	Full+	Full+	Full	Full	Full+
Dates and Times	Full+	Full	Full+	Full+	Full+
Functions	Full	Full	Full	Full	None
Math	Full+	Full+	Full+	Full	Full+
Random	None	None	None	None	Full
Sets	Full	Full	Full	Full	Full
Dynamic	+	+	+	None	None
Regular Expressions	+	None	None	None	+
Strings	+	+	+	None	+

a This describes Saxon 6.5.3 (for XSLT 1.0). Version 8.x (for XSLT 2.0) adds full support for the Random module as well as additional Math function implementations. Also, some extensions have been withdrawn in 8.x, supplanted by their XSLT 2.0 counterparts.

Use this legend for interpreting Table 15:

Full
> All core functions and/or elements are implemented.

+
> One or more optional functions or elements are implemented.

None
> No functions or elements are implemented.

Processor support for individual optional extensions is listed in the following reference.

EXSLT also provides a library of named templates and functions implemented in XSLT that correspond to many of the extensions it defines. These are individually available for download at *http://www.exslt.org*. The named templates are based on pure XSLT 1.0, so they will work with any XSLT processor. The function implementations work only if the processor supports EXSLT's func:function element. The following reference indicates which template and function implementations are available from each module.

EXSLT—Common

The EXSLT Common module consists of two core functions and one optional element. The namespace for this module is http://exslt.org/common, and the conventional namespace prefix is exsl.

Core Functions—Common Module

The following processors support EXSLT—Common (i.e., all the core extensions):

☑ 4XSLT   ☑ libxslt   ☑ Xalan-J   ☑ Saxon   ☑ EXSLT.NET

Xalan-C++ also claims experimental support for functions in this module.

node-set exsl:node-set(*object*)

This function converts a result tree fragment to a node-set that contains one root node. (A result tree fragment is what you get when you use the content of xsl:variable instead of its select attribute to define a variable.) This enables you to process the XML that you create within a variable, and therefore do multistep processing.

If the argument is a node-set, then it is returned as is. If the argument is of any other type (string, number, or boolean), then it is converted to a string; a node-set consisting of a single text node with that string as its string-value is returned.

For example, exsl:node-set($rtf)/node( ) converts the $rtf variable to a first-class node-set and then selects the children of that root node. See the "Result Tree Fragments" section in Chapter 2.

TIP

The exsl:node-set( ) function is no longer necessary in XSLT 2.0, which provides native support for "temporary trees" as first-class node-sets.

---

string exsl:object-type(*object*)

This function returns a string that indicates the type of the argument passed to it. The possible object types are: string, number, boolean, node-set, RTF, or external.

For example:

    exsl:object-type("foo")

returns string, and exsl:object-type(35) returns number.

TIP

Compare XPath 2.0's built-in instance of operator.

Optional Elements—Common Module

There is currently just one optional element in the Common module, exsl:document. These processors support the exsl:document element:

☑ 4XSLT   ☑ libxslt   ☐ Xalan-J   ☐ Saxon   ☑ EXSLT.NET

TIP

The open source Sablotron XSLT processor (*http://www.gingerall.org*) also supports exsl:document.

`<exsl:document>`

```
<exsl:document
    href = { uri-reference }
    method = { "xml" | "html" | "text" |
        qname-but-not-ncname }
    version = { nmtoken }
    encoding = { string }
    omit-xml-declaration = { "yes" | "no" }
    standalone = { "yes" | "no" }
    doctype-public = { string }
    doctype-system = { string }
    cdata-section-elements = { qnames }
    indent = { "yes" | "no" }
    media-type = { string }>
    <!-- Content: template -->
</exsl:document>
```

The `exsl:document` instruction is used to create a secondary result document in addition to the main result tree. The content of the `exsl:document` element is a template, which is instantiated to create the secondary document. The `href` attribute specifies where the secondary document should be stored. Its value must be an absolute or relative URI, and it must not include a fragment identifier.

The remaining attributes on `exsl:document` are applied to the secondary result document in the same way that the attributes on `xsl:output` are applied to the main result document.

For example, the following creates a main result document specifying an HTML frameset with two frames, together with two secondary documents, one for the content of each frame:

```
<xsl:template match="/">
  <html>
    <head><title>Frame example</title></head>
    <frameset cols="20%, 80%">
      <frame src="toc.html"/>
      <exsl:document href="toc.html">
        <html>
          <head><title>Table of Contents</title> </head>
```

```
            <body>
                <xsl:apply-templates mode="toc" select="*"/>
            </body>
        </html>
    </exsl:document>
    <frame src="body.html"/>
    <exsl:document href="body.html">
        <html>
            <head><title>Body</title></head>
            <body>
                <xsl:apply-templates select="*"/>
            </body>
        </html>
    </exsl:document>
        </frameset>
    </html>
</xsl:template>
```

TIP

Compare XSLT 2.0's `xsl:result-document` instruction.

EXSLT—Dates and Times

The Dates and Times module consists of 18 core functions, 9
optional functions, and 1 optional element. The namespace
for this module is `http://exslt.org/dates-and-times`, and
the conventional namespace prefix is date.

Data Types

The format of date-related string arguments to functions in
this module must conform to the constraints laid out in
"XML Schema Part 2: Data Types" (*http://www.w3.org/TR/
xmlschema-2/*). Generally, if an argument does not conform
to the expected type, the function does not throw an error.
Instead, it returns an empty string if its return type is string,
or NaN if its return type is number. Table 16 shows the basic
format of each data type used in the EXSLT Dates and Times

---

module. Except for xs:duration, each can also be followed by an optional time zone indicator.

Table 16. XML Schema date-related data types

XML Schema data type	Lexical representation
xs:dateTime	*CCYY-MM-DDThh:mm:ss[.sss]*
xs:date	*CCYY-MM-DD*
xs:time	*Hh:mm:ss[.sss]*
xs:gYearMonth	*CCYY-MM*
xs:gYear	*CCYY*
xs:gMonth	*--MM--*
xs:gMonthDay	*--MM-DD*
xs:gDay	*---DD*
xs:duration	*[-]PnYnMnDTnHnMnS*

TIP

XPath 2.0 introduces all of these data types as first-class data types in the language, along with functions and operators for working with them.

Core Functions—Dates and Times Module

The following processors support EXSLT—Dates and Times (i.e., all the core extensions):

☑ 4XSLT   ☑ libxslt   ☑ Xalan-J   ☑ Saxon   ☑ EXSLT.NET

Xalan-C++ also claims experimental support for functions in this module.

All core Dates and Times functions, except for date:date-time( ), are also implemented as XSLT templates and EXSLT functions. Download them from *http://www.exslt.org/date/*.

string date:date(*string?*)

> This function returns the date part of the date/time argument string. The format of the argument must be either xs:dateTime or xs:date. When absent, the argument defaults to the current date/time string. The returned string is in the xs:date format (*CCYY-MM-DD*).
>
> For example:
>
> > date:date("2005-05-01T12:30:59")
>
> returns the string:
>
> > 2005-05-01

string date:date-time( )

> This function returns the current date and time as a date/time string in the xs:dateTime format (*CCYY-MM-DDThh:mm:ss*).
>
> For example, on May 1st, 2005, at noon, the date:date-time( ) function would return the string 2005-05-01T12:00:00.

TIP

Compare XPath 2.0's built-in function current-dateTime( ).

---

string date:day-abbreviation(*string?*)

> This function returns the three-letter English abbreviation of the day of the week of a date. The format of the argument must be either xs:dateTime or xs:date. When absent, the argument defaults to the current date/time string.
>
> For example, date:day-abbreviation("2005-05-01") returns the string Sun, and date:day-abbreviation("2005-12-31") returns the string Sat.

number date:day-in-month(*string?*)

> This function returns the day of a date as a number. The format of the argument must be one of xs:dateTime, xs:date, xs:gMonthDay, or xs:gDay. When absent, the argument defaults to the current date/time string.

For example, date:day-in-month("2005-05-01") returns the number 1, and date:day-in-month("2005-12-31") returns the number 31.

TIP

Compare XPath 2.0's built-in functions day-from-dateTime( ) and day-from-date( ).

---

number date:day-in-week(*string?*)

This function returns the day of the week given in a date as a number. The numbering of days in the week starts at 1 for Sunday, 2 for Monday, up to 7 for Saturday. The format of the argument must be either xs:dateTime or xs:date. When absent, the argument defaults to the current date/time string.

For example, date:day-in-week("2005-05-01") returns the number 1 (for Sunday), and date:day-in-week("2005-12-31") returns the number 7 (for Saturday).

number date:day-in-year(*string?*)

This function returns the day of the year in the given date as a number. The format of the argument must be either xs:dateTime or xs:date. When absent, the argument defaults to the current date/time string.

For example, date:day-in-year("2005-05-01") returns the number 121, and date:day-in-year("2005-12-31") returns the number 365.

string date:day-name(*string?*)

This function returns the full English name of the day of the week of a date. The format of the argument must be either xs:dateTime or xs:date. When absent, the argument defaults to the current date/time string.

For example, date:day-name("2005-05-01") returns the string Sunday, and date:day-name("2005-12-31") returns the string Saturday.

number date:day-of-week-in-month(*string?*)

> This function returns the day of the week in a month of a date as a number. The format of the argument must be either xs:dateTime or xs:date. When absent, the argument defaults to the current date/time string.

> For example, date:day-of-week-in-month("2005-05-01") returns the number 1 (for the 1st Sunday of the month), and date:day-of-week-in-month("2005-12-31") returns the number 5 (for the 5th Saturday of the month).

number date:hour-in-day(*string?*)

> This function returns the hour of the day as a number. The format of the argument must be either xs:dateTime or xs:time. When absent, the argument defaults to the current date/time string.

> For example, date:hour-in-day("16:45:05") returns the number 16, and date:hour-in-day("2006-01-01T03:30:59") returns the number 3.

TIP

Compare XPath 2.0's built-in functions hours-from-dateTime( ) and hours-from-time( ).

---

boolean date:leap-year(*string?*)

> This function returns true if the year given in a date is a leap year. The format of the argument must be one of xs:dateTime, xs:date, xs:gYearMonth, or xs:gYear. When absent, the argument defaults to the current date/time string.

> For example, date:leap-year("2004-09") returns true because 2004 was a leap year. On the other hand, date:leap-year("2003-05-01T09:22:00") returns false because 2003 was not a leap year.

number date:minute-in-hour(*string?*)

This function returns the minute of the hour as a number. The format of the argument must be either xs:dateTime or xs:time. When absent, the argument defaults to the current date/time string.

For example, date:minute-in-hour("16:45:05") returns the number 45, and date:minute-in-hour("2006-01-01T03:30:59") returns the number 30.

TIP

Compare XPath 2.0's built-in functions minutes-from-dateTime( ) and minutes-from-time( ).

---

string date:month-abbreviation(*string?*)

This function returns the three-letter English abbreviation of the month of a date. The format of the argument must be one of xs:dateTime, xs:date, xs:gYearMonth, xs:gMonth, or xs:gMonthDay. When absent, the argument defaults to the current date/time string.

For example, date:month-abbreviation("2005-06") returns the string Jun, and date:month-name("2005-09-02T12:00:00") returns the string Sep.

number date:month-in-year(*string?*)

This function returns the month of a date as a number. The format of the argument must be one of xs:dateTime, xs:date, xs:gYearMonth, xs:gMonth, or xs:gMonthDay. When absent, the argument defaults to the current date/time string.

For example, date:month-in-year("2005-05") returns the number 5.

TIP

Compare XPath 2.0's built-in functions month-from-dateTime( ) and month-from-date( ).

---

string date:month-name(*string?*)

This function returns the full English name of the month of a date. The format of the argument must be one of xs:dateTime, xs:date, xs:gYearMonth, xs:gMonth, or xs:gMonthDay. When absent, the argument defaults to the current date/time string.

For example, date:month-name("2005-06") returns the string June, and date:month-name("2005-09-02T12:00:00") returns the string September.

number date:second-in-minute(*string?*)

This function returns the second of the minute as a number. The format of the argument must be either xs:dateTime or xs:time. When absent, the argument defaults to the current date/time string.

For example, date:second-in-minute("16:45:05") returns the number 5, and date:second-in-minute("2006-01-01T03:30:59") returns the number 59.

TIP

Compare XPath 2.0's built-in functions seconds-from-dateTime( ) and seconds-from-time( ).

---

string date:time(*string?*)

This function returns the time part of the date/time argument string. The format of the argument must be either xs:dateTime or xs:time. When absent, the argument defaults to the current date/time string. The returned string is in the xs:time format (*hh*:*mm*:*ss*).

For example, date:time("2005-05-01T12:30:59") returns the string 12:30:59.

number date:week-in-year(*string?*)

This function returns the week of the year in the given date as a number. The format of the argument must be either xs:dateTime or xs:date. When absent, the argument defaults to the current date/time string.

For example, date:week-in-year("2005-05-01") returns the number 17, and date:week-in-year("2005-12-31") returns the number 52.

number date:year(*string?*)

This function returns the year of a date as a number. The format of the argument must be one of xs:dateTime, xs:date, xs:gYearMonth, or xs:gYear. When absent, the argument defaults to the current date/time string.

For example, date:year("2005-05-01T12:30:59") returns the number 2005.

TIP

Compare XPath 2.0's built-in functions year-from-dateTime( ) and year-from-date( ).

Optional Functions—Dates and Times Module

All of the optional Dates and Times functions, except for date:parse-date( ), date:sum( ), and date:seconds( ), are also implemented as XSLT templates and EXSLT functions. Download them from *http://www.exslt.org/date/*.

string date:add(*string, string*)

This function returns the date/time resulting from adding a duration (the second argument) to a date/time (the first argument). The format of the first argument must be one of xs:dateTime, xs:date, xs:gYearMonth, or xs:gYear. The format of the second argument must conform to the xs:duration data type. The return value is calculated using the algorithm described in *http://www.w3.org/TR/xmlschema-2/#adding-durations-to-dateTimes*.

For example:

    date:add("2005-05-01","PT33H")

returns the string:

    2005-05-02

These processors support the date:add( ) function:

☑ 4XSLT   ☑ libxslt   ☐ Xalan-J   ☐ Saxon   ☑ EXSLT.NET

string date:add-duration(*string, string*)

This function returns the duration resulting from adding two durations together. Both arguments must conform to the xs:duration data type. The return value is calculated using the algorithm described in *http://www.w3.org/TR/xmlschema-2/#adding-durations-to-dateTimes*.

For example:

```
date:add-duration("P2DT12H5M","P5DT3H5M")
```

returns the string P7DT15H10M (7 days, 15 hours, and 10 minutes).

The following processors support the date:add-duration( ) function:

☐ 4XSLT   ☑ libxslt   ☐ Xalan-J   ☐ Saxon   ☑ EXSLT.NET

string date:difference(*string, string*)

This function returns the duration between the first date and the second date. If the first date occurs before the second date, then the result is a positive duration; if it occurs after the second date, the result is a negative duration. The format of the arguments must be among these: xs:dateTime, xs:date, xs:gYearMonth, and xs:gYear. The returned string conforms to the xs:duration format.

For example:

```
date:difference("2005-10-30", "2005-10-15")
```

returns the string:

```
-P15D
```

TIP

Compare XPath 2.0's polymorphic minus (-) operator when applied to date/time values.

The following processors support the date:difference( ) function:

☑ 4XSLT   ☑ libxslt   ☐ Xalan-J   ☐ Saxon   ☑ EXSLT.NET

string date:duration(*number?*)

This function returns an xs:duration string (days, hours, minutes, and seconds only) representing the number of seconds specified by the argument string. If no argument is given, then the result of calling date:seconds( ) without any arguments is used as a default argument.

For example, date:duration(60) returns the string PT1M (one minute), and date:duration(6000) returns PT1H40M. The date:duration( ) function complements the date: seconds( ) function. For example, date:duration(date: seconds("P1D")) returns P1D.

The following processors support the date:duration( ) function:

☐ 4XSLT   ☑ libxslt   ☐ Xalan-J   ☐ Saxon   ☑ EXSLT.NET

string date:format-date(*string, string*)

This function formats the date/time in the first argument according to the pattern in the second argument. The format of the first argument must be one of xs:dateTime, xs:date, xs:time, xs:gYearMonth, xs:gYear, xs:gMonthDay, xs:gMonth, or xs:gDay. The second argument is a format pattern that must be in the syntax specified by the JDK 1.1 SimpleDateFormat class and is interpreted as described for the JDK 1.1 SimpleDateFormat class.

If the date/time format of the first argument is right truncated (i.e., in a format other than xs:time or xs:dateTime), then any missing components are assumed to be as follows: if no month is specified, it is given a month of 01; if no day is specified, it is given a day of 01; if no time is specified, it is given a time of 00:00:00.

If the date/time format of the first argument is left truncated (i.e., xs:time, xs:gMonthDay, xs:gMonth, or xs:gDay), and the format pattern has a token that uses a component that is missing from the date/time format used, then that token is replaced with an empty string within the result.

For example:

```
date:format-date('2005-12-31','MM/DD/YY')
```

returns the string:

```
12/31/05
```

TIP

Compare XSLT 2.0's built-in functions format-dateTime( ), format-date( ), and format-time( ).

The following processors support the date:format-date( ) function:

☐ 4XSLT   ☐ libxslt   ☑ Xalan-J   ☐ Saxon   ☑ EXSLT.NET

string date:parse-date(*string, string*)

This function parses the string in the first argument according to the date/time pattern given in the second argument. The second argument is a format pattern that must be in the syntax specified by the JDK 1.1 Simple-DateFormat class and is interpreted as described for the JDK 1.1 SimpleDateFormat class. The interpreted date is

---

returned as a string in one of these formats: `xs:dateTime`, `xs:date`, `xs:time`, `xs:gYearMonth`, `xs:gYear`, `xs:gMonthDay`, `xs:gMonth`, or `xs:gDay`.

The interpreted date is formatted to the least specific format as possible, providing that all the components specified for it are represented within the result. If the format includes a component that is not specified within the interpreted date, then these components are given default values as follows: year defaults to 0001; month and day default to 01; hour, minute, and second default to 00.

For example:

```
date:parse-date('12/31/05','MM/DD/YY')
```

returns the string :

```
2005-12-31
```

The following processors support the `date:parse-date()` function:

☐ 4XSLT   ☐ libxslt   ☐ Xalan-J   ☐ Saxon   ☑ EXSLT.NET

number `date:seconds(`*string?*`)`

This function returns the number of seconds in the duration supplied (or implied) by the argument string. The argument format must be one of `xs:dateTime`, `xs:date`, `xs:gYearMonth`, `xs:gYear`, or `xs:duration`. When absent, the argument defaults to the current date/time string.

If the argument is in the `xs:duration` format, then the duration string must be specified in days, hours, minutes, and seconds only. (The number of years and months must be set to zero if present in the string.) The number returned is the result of converting the duration to seconds by assuming that 1 day = 24 hours, 1 hour = 60 minutes and 1 minute = 60 seconds.

If the argument is in one of the other formats, then the difference between the date/time string and 1970-01-01T00:00:00Z is calculated as with `date:difference()`, and the resulting duration is converted to seconds as just described.

The following processors support the date:seconds() function:

☑ 4XSLT   ☑ libxslt   ☐ Xalan-J   ☐ Saxon   ☑ EXSLT.NET

string date:sum(*node-set*)

> This function adds a set of durations together. The string-values of the nodes in the argument node-set are interpreted as xs:duration strings and added together as if by calling the date:add-duration() function.

> For example, date:sum(/durations/duration) interprets the string-value of each duration element as an xs:duration string and sums it with all of the other duration values.

TIP

Compare XPath 2.0's polymorphic plus (+) operator when applied to duration values.

These processors support the date:sum() function:

☐ 4XSLT   ☑ libxslt   ☐ Xalan-J   ☐ Saxon   ☑ EXSLT.NET

number date:week-in-month(*string?*)

> This function returns the week in the month of the given date as a number. For the purposes of numbering, the first day of the month is in week 1, and new weeks begin on a Monday (so the first and last weeks in a month will often have less than 7 days in them). The format of the argument must be either xs:dateTime or xs:date. When absent, the argument defaults to the current date/time string.

> For example, date:week-in-month('2005-10-03') returns the number 2 because the 3rd of October 2005 is a Monday, which begins the second week.

These processors support the `date:week-in-month()` function:

☐ 4XSLT ☑ libxslt ☐ Xalan-J ☑ Saxon ☑ EXSLT.NET

Optional Elements—Dates and Times Module

The `date:date-format` element is defined at *http://exslt.org/date/elements/date-format/*. No known implementations were available at the time of this writing.

EXSLT—Functions

The Functions module consists of two core elements and one optional element. The namespace for this module is `http://exslt.org/functions`, and the conventional namespace prefix is `func`.

Core Elements—Functions Module

The following processors support EXSLT—Functions (i.e., all the core extensions):

☑ 4XSLT ☑ libxslt ☑ Xalan-J ☑ Saxon ☐ EXSLT.NET

<func:function>

```
<func:function
   name = qname>
   <!-- Content: (xsl:param* | template) -->
</func:function>
```

The `func:function` element is a top-level extension element that enables users to define their own functions. The `name` attribute denotes the name of the function, which must include a namespace prefix. A `func:function` definition with the same name as an imported `func:function` definition (using `xsl:import`) overrides the imported definition.

Function parameters are defined using zero or more xsl: param elements, according to their relative position. In a function call, the first argument is assigned to the first parameter, the second to the second, and so on. Each xsl:param element indicates an expected, but optional, argument (as with xsl: param elements in named templates).

The function's return value is determined by instantiating a func:result element inside the function definition. It is an error if the instantiation of the template inside func:function results in the generation of result nodes, other than inside the func:result element. If no func:result element is instantiated, the function will return an empty string.

For example, this function declares one parameter:

```
<func:function name="my:func">
  <xsl:param name="var"/>
  <xsl:if test="$var='please'">
    <func:result select="'thanks'"/>
  </xsl:if>
</func:function>
```

Given the above function definition, my:func("please") will return the string thanks, but my:func() or my: func("anything") will return an empty string because, in those cases, no func:result element is instantiated.

The following example is invalid because it tries to create a result node outside the func:result element:

```
<func:function name="my:func2">
  <foo/> <!-- wrong -->
</func:function>
```

TIP

Compare XSLT 2.0's built-in top-level element xsl: function.

`<func:result>`

```
<func:result
  select = expression>
  <!-- Content: template -->
</func:result>
```

The func:result element is used to return a value from within a function definition. It may occur only as a descendant of the func:function element, and it may not have any following siblings other than xsl:fallback. Its value is determined in the same way that variable and parameter values are determined using xsl:variable and xsl:param:

- If the select attribute is present, then the func:result element must be empty, and the value of the select expression is used as the return value.

- If the select attribute is absent and the func:result element has nonempty content (i.e., it has one or more child nodes), then the content of the func:result element is instantiated to return a result tree fragment.

- If the select attribute is absent and the func:result is empty, then the return value is an empty string.

For example, the following function definition will return a boolean, result tree fragment, or empty string, depending on what argument is passed to it:

```
<func:function name="my:pick">
  <xsl:param name="x"/>
  <xsl:choose>
    <xsl:when test="$x = 'bool'">
      <func:result select="true()"/> <!-- boolean -->
    </xsl:when>
    <xsl:when test="$x = 'rtf'">
      <func:result>
        <foo/>        <!-- result tree fragment -->
      </func:result>
    </xsl:when>
    <xsl:otherwise>
      <func:result/> <!-- empty string -->
    </xsl:otherwise>
  </xsl:choose>
</func:function>
```

Given the above function definition, `my:pick('bool')` returns boolean true, `my:pick('rtf')` returns a result tree fragment, and `my:pick( )` with any other argument—or no argument at all—returns an empty string.

TIP

XSLT 2.0 does not have a direct counterpart to EXSLT's `func:result` element, as `xsl:function` does not have the same content restrictions as `func:function`. However, XSLT 2.0's `xsl:sequence` instruction is useful for returning nodes and other sequences as the result of a user-defined function.

Optional Elements—Functions Module

There is currently just one optional element in the Functions module, `func:script`. The `func:script` element is not supported by any of the five XSLT processors featured in this reference. However, the Sablotron XSLT processor (*http://www. gingerall.org*) supports JavaScript extensions using a flavor of `func:script` (which does not conform exactly to the EXSLT definition).

\<func:script>

```
<func:script
   implements-prefix = ncname
   language = qname-and-not-ncname
   src = uri-reference
   archive = uri-reference />
```

The `func:script` element is based historically on the abandoned `xsl:script` element from the defunct XSLT 1.1 specification (*http://www.w3.org/TR/xslt11*). It is a top-level extension element designed to enable other scripting languages to be embedded into XSLT. Here is an example script definition:

```
<func:script language="javascript"
    implements-prefix="my">
  function sayHi() { return "Hi"; }
</func:script>
```

Given this definition, the my:sayHi() function can be called from within XSLT, returning the string Hi.

EXSLT—Math

The Math module consists of four core functions and 14 optional functions. The namespace for this module is http://exslt.org/math, and the conventional namespace prefix is math.

Core Functions—Math Module

The following processors support EXSLT—Math (i.e., all the core extensions):

☑ 4XSLT ☑ libxslt ☑ Xalan-J ☑ Saxon ☑ EXSLT.NET

Xalan-C++ also claims experimental support for functions in this module.

All core Math functions are also implemented as XSLT templates and EXSLT functions. Download them from *http://www.exslt.org/math/*.

node-set math:highest(*node-set*)
> This function returns all of the nodes in the argument node-set that have the maximum value for the node-set, as if calculated by math:max( ). A node has the maximum value if the result of converting its string-value to a number is equal to the maximum value.

node-set math:lowest(*node-set*)
> This function returns all of the nodes in the argument node-set that have the minimum value for the node-set, as if calculated by math:min( ). A node has the minimum

value if the result of converting its string-value to a number is equal to the minimum value.

number math:max(*node-set*)

> This function returns the maximum value of the nodes in the argument node-set. This is computed first by sorting the node-set in descending order as if by using xsl:sort in this way:
>
> ```
> <xsl:sort data-type="number" order="descending"/>
> ```
>
> The string-value of the first node in this sorted list is then converted to a number as if by calling the number( ) function. The result is the maximum value.
>
> If the node-set is empty, or if the result of converting the string-values of any of the nodes to a number is NaN, then NaN is returned.

TIP

Compare XPath 2.0's built-in function max( ).

---

number math:min(*node-set*)

> This function returns the minimum value of the nodes in the argument node-set. This is computed first by sorting the node-set in ascending order as if by using xsl:sort in this way:
>
> ```
> <xsl:sort data-type="number" order="ascending"/>
> ```
>
> The string-value of the first node in this sorted list is then converted to a number as if by calling the number( ) function. The result is the minimum value.
>
> If the node-set is empty, or if the result of converting the string-values of any of the nodes to a number is NaN, then NaN is returned.

TIP

Compare XPath 2.0's built-in function min( ).

Optional Functions—Math Module

The following processors support all of the optional Math functions listed next:

☑ 4XSLT ☑ libxslt ☑ Xalan-J ☑ Saxon ☑ EXSLT.NET

Three of the optional Math functions are also implemented as XSLT templates and EXSLT functions: math:constant( ), math:power( ), and math:sqrt( ). Download them from *http://www.exslt.org/math/*.

number math:abs(*number*)

This function returns the absolute value of a number. For example, math:abs(-3) returns 3.

TIP

Compare XPath 2.0's built-in function abs( ).

---

number math:acos(*number*)

This function returns the arccosine of a number in radians.

number math:asin(*number*)

This function returns the arcsine of a number in radians.

number math:atan(*number*)

This function returns the arctangent of a number in radians.

number math:atan2(*number, number*)

This function returns the angle in radians from the x-axis to a point (*x,y*), where *x* is the first argument, and *y* is the second argument.

number math:constant(*string, number*)

This function returns the specified constant to a set precision. The possible constants are: PI, E, SQRRT2, LN2, LN10, LOG2E, and SQRT1_2. The second argument specifies the precision in terms of how many characters should appear in the number converted to a string, including the decimal point.

For example, math:constant("PI",10) returns the number 3.14159265 because 3.14159265 is 10 characters long.

number math:cos(*number*)
> This function returns the cosine of a number in radians.

number math:exp(*number*)
> This function returns **e** (the base of natural logarithms) raised to a power. The constant **e** is Euler's constant, approximately equal to 2.178.

number math:log(*number*)
> This function returns the natural logarithm of a number; the base is **e**.

number math:power(*number, number*)
> This function returns the value of a base expression taken to a specified power. For example, math:power(2,5) returns 32 (2^5).

number math:random( )
> This function returns a random number from 0 to 1. See also random:random-sequence( ) later in this chapter.

number math:sin(*number*)
> This function returns the sine of a number in radians.

number math:sqrt(*number*)
> This function returns the square root of a number. If the argument is a negative number, the return value is 0.

number math:tan(*number*)
> This function returns the tangent of a number in radians.

EXSLT—Random

The Random module consists of just one core function. The namespace for this module is http://exslt.org/random, and the conventional namespace prefix is random.

Core Functions—Random Module

The following processors support EXSLT—Random:

☐ 4XSLT ☐ libxslt ☐ Xalan-J ☑ Saxon (8.1) ☑ EXSLT.NET

number+ random:random-sequence(*number?, number?*)

This function returns a sequence of random numbers between 0 and 1. The first argument indicates how many random numbers to generate. When absent, it defaults to 1. The second argument is an optional seed number. When absent, it defaults to a value derived from the current date/time.

What a "sequence of numbers" means depends on which processor you are using. The only kind of "sequence" that XSLT 1.0 supports is a node-set, so if you're using EXSLT.NET, then the return value will be a node-set consisting of one or more sibling random elements, each containing a random number.

On the other hand, XSLT/XPath 2.0 supports ordered sequences of simple values, so if you're using Saxon 8.1 or higher, then the return value will be an actual sequence of numbers, rather than a node-set.

For example, the following stylesheet outputs different results, depending on whether you're using EXSLT.NET or Saxon 8.1 or higher:

```
<xsl:stylesheet version="1.0"
  xmlns:xsl="http://www.w3.org/1999/XSL/Transform"
  xmlns:random="http://exslt.org/random"
  exclude-result-prefixes="random">

<xsl:output indent="yes" omit-xml-declaration="yes"/>

<xsl:template match="/">
  <xsl:copy-of select="random:random-sequence(3)"/>
</xsl:template>

</xsl:stylesheet>
```

Executing this stylesheet with *nxslt.exe* (which bundles the EXSLT.NET library) results in output that looks like this:

```
<random>0.649705002852578</random>
<random>0.559270384981889</random>
<random>0.570297354632196</random>
```

On the other hand, Saxon 8.1 (or higher) outputs something like this:

```
0.06550816273681126 0.007289242615926783 0.
3906861986281809
```

EXSLT—Sets

The Sets module consists of six core functions. The namespace for this module is http://exslt.org/sets, and the conventional namespace prefix is set.

Core Functions—Sets Module

The following processors support EXSLT—Sets:

☑ 4XSLT ☑ libxslt ☑ Xalan-J ☑ Saxon ☑ EXSLT.NET

Xalan-C++ also claims experimental support for functions in this module.

All core Sets functions are also implemented as XSLT templates and EXSLT functions. Download them from *http://www.exslt.org/sets/*.

node-set set:difference(*node-set, node-set*)
> This function returns the difference between two node-sets, i.e., those nodes that are in the first argument that are not in the second argument.

TIP

Compare XPath 2.0's built-in except operator.

---

node-set set:distinct(*node-set*)

This function returns a subset of the nodes contained in the node-set argument. It selects a node if there is no other node that has the same string-value and that precedes it in document order.

This function is useful in grouping-related problems. For example, the following code uses set:distinct() to iterate over each unique country once, in order to group cities by their country:

```
<xsl:for-each select="set:distinct(//city/@country)">
  <country name="{.}">
    <xsl:copy-of select="//city[@country=current()]">
  </country>
</xsl:for-each>
```

TIP

Compare XPath 2.0's built-in function distinct-values(). Also, compare XSLT 2.0's xsl:for-each-group element.

boolean set:has-same-node(*node-set, node-set*)

This function returns true if the two argument node-sets share any nodes, and false otherwise.

TIP

Compare XPath 2.0's built-in intersect operator in conjunction with its built-in function exists().

node-set set:intersection(*node-set, node-set*)

This function returns the intersection of two node-sets, i.e., only those nodes that are present in both argument node-sets.

TIP

Compare XPath 2.0's built-in intersect operator.

node-set set:leading(*node-set, node-set*)

This function returns the nodes in the first argument node-set that precede, in document order, the first node in the second argument node-set. If the first node in the second node-set is not contained in the first node-set, then an empty node-set is returned. If the second node-set is empty, the first node-set is returned.

TIP

Compare XPath 2.0's built-in "node-before" operator (<<), as in A[. << B].

---

node-set set:trailing(*node-set, node-set*)

This function returns the nodes in the first argument node-set that follow, in document order, the first node in the second argument node-set. If the first node in the second node-set is not contained in the first node-set, then an empty node-set is returned. If the second node-set is empty, the first node-set is returned.

TIP

Compare XPath 2.0's built-in "node-after" operator (>>), as in A[. >> B].

EXSLT—Dynamic

The Dynamic module consists of six optional functions. The namespace for this module is http://exslt.org/dynamic, and the conventional namespace prefix is dyn.

Xalan-C++ claims experimental support for functions in this module. Support information for the XSLT processors featured in this chapter is included individually with each upcoming function.

Optional Functions—Dynamic Module

node-set dyn:closure(*node-set, string*)

This function returns a node-set resulting from the transitive closure of evaluating the expression string passed as the second argument on each of the nodes in the first argument node-set, and then on the node-set resulting from that, and so on until no more nodes are found.

For example, dyn:closure(., '*') returns all the descendant elements of the context node (its element children, their children, their children's children, and so on).

The expression in the second argument is thus evaluated several times, each with a different node acting as the context of the expression. The first time the expression is evaluated, the first argument passed to the dyn:closure( ) function supplies the context. In other words, for each node in the first argument, the XPath expression is evaluated with all context information being the same as that for the call to the dyn:closure( ) function itself, except for the following:

- The context node is the node being iterated over.
- The context position is the position of the context node within the node-set passed as the first argument, arranged in document order.
- The context size is the number of nodes in the first argument node-set.

The result for a particular iteration is the union of the node-sets resulting from evaluating the expression for each of the nodes in the source node-set for that iteration. This result is then used as the source node-set for the next iteration, and so on. The result of the function as a whole is the union of the node-sets generated by each iteration.

If the expression string passed as the second argument is an invalid XPath expression (including an empty string) or an expression that does not return a node-set, then the function returns an empty node-set.

Here is another example use of this function (that can't be reformulated using other XPath features):

```
dyn:closure(graph/node, 'id(@idref)')
```

This function call will effectively retrieve all the nodes in a graph represented using ID references within a document. The `dyn:closure()` function is necessary because you may not know *a priori* how many IDREF traversals you will need to make to select all nodes in the graph, and so nested calls to `id()` will not suffice.

TIP

In XSLT 2.0, you can implement your own transitive closures by writing a recursive function definition, provided that the expression is statically available (not constructed dynamically as allowed by `dyn:closure()`).

The following processors support the `dyn:closure()` function:

☐ 4XSLT ☐ libxslt ☑ Xalan-J ☐ Saxon ☐ EXSLT.NET

object `dyn:evaluate(string)`

This function evaluates a string as an XPath expression and returns the resulting value, which might be a boolean, number, string, node-set, result tree fragment, or external object. The sole argument is the string to be evaluated.

The string is always evaluated exactly as if it had been literally included in place of the call to the `dyn:evaluate()` function. For example:

```
<xsl:value-of select="dyn:evaluate('foo:bar')"/>
```

Creates a text node with exactly the same value as:

```
<xsl:value-of select="foo:bar"/>
```

In other words, the context used when evaluating the XPath expression is exactly the same as the context used when evaluating the dyn:evaluate( ) function.

If the expression string passed as the second argument is an invalid XPath expression (including an empty string), then the function returns an empty node-set.

You should only use this function if the expression must be constructed dynamically. Otherwise, it is much more efficient to use the expression literally.

TIP

XPath 2.0 provides no built-in support for dynamic expression evaluation.

The following processors support the dyn:evaluate( ) function:

☑ 4XSLT   ☑ libxslt   ☑ Xalan-J   ☐ Saxon   ☐ EXSLT.NET

node-set dyn:map(*node-set, string*)

This function evaluates the expression passed as the second argument for each of the nodes passed as the first argument, and it returns a node-set that represents all of the resulting values.

The expression is evaluated relative to the nodes passed as the first argument.

In other words, for each node in the first argument, the XPath expression is evaluated with all context information being the same as that for the call to the dyn:map( ) function itself, except for the following:

- The context node is the node being iterated over.
- The context position is the position of the node within the node-set passed as the first argument, arranged in document order.
- The context size is the number of nodes in the first argument node-set.

If the expression string passed as the second argument is an invalid XPath expression (including an empty string), then the function returns an empty node-set.

If the XPath expression evaluates to a node-set, the dyn: map( ) function returns the union of the node-sets returned from evaluating the expression for each of the nodes in the first argument. Note that this may mean that the node-set resulting from the call to the dyn:map( ) function contains a different number of nodes than the number in the node-set passed as the first argument.

If the XPath expression evaluates to a number, the dyn: map( ) function returns a node-set containing one exsl: number element (namespace http://exslt.org/common) for each node in the node-set passed as the first argument, in document order. The string-value of each exsl:number element is the same as the result of converting the number resulting from evaluating the expression to a string as with the number function, with the exception that Infinity results in an exsl:number element holding the highest number the implementation can store, and –Infinity results in an exsl:number element holding the lowest number the implementation can store.

If the XPath expression evaluates to a boolean, the dyn: map( ) function returns a node-set containing one exsl: boolean element (namespace http://exslt.org/common) for each node in the node-set passed as the first argument, in document order. The string-value of each exsl: boolean element is true, if the expression evaluates to true, and "" (empty string), if the expression evaluates to false.

Otherwise, the dyn:map( ) function returns a node-set containing one exsl:string element (namespace http:// exslt.org/common) for each node in the node-set passed as the first argument to the dyn:map( ) function, in document order. The string-value of each exsl:string element is the same as the result of converting the result of evaluating the expression for the relevant node to a string, as if by calling the `string()` function.

TIP

Compare `for` expressions in XPath 2.0, which allow you to evaluate an arbitrary expression for each item in a sequence, returning the union of the results. The only limitation is that, unlike the `dyn:map()` function, the expression must be a literal expression and not a dynamically computed string.

These processors support the `dyn:map()` function:

☐ 4XSLT   ☐ libxslt   ☑ Xalan-J   ☐ Saxon   ☐ EXSLT.NET

number dyn:max(`node-set, string`)

This function calculates a maximum value for the node-set passed as the first argument, where the value for each node is calculated dynamically using an XPath expression string passed as the second argument.

For each node in the first argument, the XPath expression is evaluated with all context information being the same as that for the call to the `dyn:max()` function itself, except for the following:

- The context node is the node being iterated over.
- The context position is the position of the node within the node-set passed as the first argument, arranged in document order.
- The context size is the number of nodes in the first argument node-set.

This function returns the maximum of these values, calculated in exactly the same way as for `math:max()`.

If the expression string passed as the second argument is an invalid XPath expression (including an empty string), this function returns NaN.

This function must take a second argument. To calculate the maximum of a set of nodes based on their string-values, you should use the math:max( ) function instead.

TIP

In XPath 2.0, you can do substantially the same thing as the dyn:max( ) function by using a for expression to create a sequence of numbers and then applying the built-in max( ) function to the resulting sequence. The only limitation is that, unlike the dyn:max( ) function, the expression within the for expression must be a literal expression and not a dynamically computed string.

These processors support the dyn:max( ) function:

☐ 4XSLT   ☐ libxslt   ☑ Xalan-J   ☐ Saxon   ☐ EXSLT.NET

number dyn:min(*node-set, string*)

This function calculates a minimum value for the node-set passed as the first argument, where the value for each node is calculated dynamically using an XPath expression string passed as the second argument.

For each node in the first argument, the XPath expression is evaluated with all context information being the same as that for the call to the dyn:min( ) function itself, except for the following:

- The context node is the node being iterated over.
- The context position is the position of the node within the node-set passed as the first argument, arranged in document order.
- The context size is the number of nodes in the first argument node-set.

This function returns the minimum of these values, calculated in exactly the same way as for math:min( ).

If the expression string passed as the second argument is an invalid XPath expression (including an empty string), this function returns NaN.

This function must take a second argument. To calculate the minimum of a set of nodes based on their string-values, you should use the math:min( ) function instead.

TIP

In XPath 2.0, you can do substantially the same thing as the dyn:min( ) function by using a for expression to create a sequence of numbers and then applying the built-in min( ) function to the resulting sequence. The only limitation is that, unlike the dyn:min( ) function, the expression within the for expression must be a literal expression and not a dynamically computed string.

These processors support the dyn:min( ) function:

☐ 4XSLT   ☐ libxslt   ☑ Xalan-J   ☐ Saxon   ☐ EXSLT.NET

number dyn:sum(*node-set, string*)

This function calculates the sum for the node-set passed as the first argument, where the value for each node is calculated dynamically using an XPath expression string passed as the second argument.

For each node in the first argument, the XPath expression is evaluated with all context information being the same as that for the call to the dyn:sum( ) function itself, except for the following:

- The context node is the node being iterated over.
- The context position is the position of the node within the node-set passed as the first argument, arranged in document order.
- The context size is the number of nodes in the first argument node-set.

This function returns the sum of these values, calculated in exactly the same way as for XPath 1.0's built-in sum( ) function.

If the expression string passed as the second argument is an invalid XPath expression (including an empty string), this function returns NaN.

This function must take a second argument. To calculate the sum of a set of nodes based on their string-values, you should use the XPath sum( ) function instead.

TIP

In XPath 2.0, you can do substantially the same thing as the dyn:sum( ) function by using a for expression to create a sequence of numbers and then applying the built-in sum( ) function to the resulting sequence. The only limitation is that, unlike the dyn:sum( ) function, the expression within the for expression must be a literal expression and not a dynamically computed string.

These processors support the dyn:sum( ) function:

☐ 4XSLT   ☐ libxslt   ☑ Xalan-J   ☐ Saxon   ☐ EXSLT.NET

EXSLT—Regular Expressions

The Regular Expressions module consists of three optional functions. The namespace for this module is http://exslt.org/regular-expressions, and the conventional namespace prefix is regexp.

Optional Functions—Regular Expressions Module

Thse processors support all of the optional Regular Expressions functions listed next:

☑ 4XSLT   ☐ libxslt   ☐ Xalan-J   ☐ Saxon   ☑ EXSLT.NET

---

object regexp:match(*string, string, string?*)

This function selects the substrings of the string passed as the first argument that match the captured parts (i.e., the parentheses-delimited parts) of the regular expression passed as the second argument. The second argument is a regular expression that follows the JavaScript regular expression syntax. The third argument is a string consisting of character flags to be used by the match. If a character is present, then that flag is true. The flags are:

g

Global match. The submatches from all the matches in the string are returned. If this character is not present, then only the submatches from the first match in the string are returned.

i

Case-insensitive. The regular expression is treated as case-insensitive. If this character is not present, then the regular expression is case-sensitive.

The function returns a node-set of match elements, each of whose string-value is equal to a portion of the first argument string that was captured by the regular expression. If the match is not global, the first match element has a value equal to the portion of the string matched by the entire regular expression.

The following example illustrates a non-global match:

```
<xsl:copy-of select="regexp:match(
    'http://example.com/foo?bar=bang#frag',
    '(\w+):\/\/([^/:]+)(:\d*)?([^# ]*)')"/>
```

that produces the following result:

```
<match>http://example.com/foo?bar=bang</match>
<match>http</match>
<match>example.com</match>
<match></match>
<match>/foo?bar=bang</match>
```

The following example illustrates a global match:

```
<xsl:copy-of select="regexp:match(
    'This is a test string','(\w+)','g')"/>
```

that produces the following result:

```
<match>This</match>
<match>is</match>
<match>a</match>
<match>test</match>
<match>string</match>
```

By contrast, here is the same example but without the g parameter:

```
<xsl:copy-of select="regexp:match(
    'This is a test string','(\w+)')"/>
```

It produces the following result:

```
<match>This</match>
<match>This</match>
```

Because it's a non-global match, the first match element contains the first substring that matches the entire regular expression (This). Because there is only one captured part of the regular expression (in parentheses), then only one submatch is returned (This).

TIP

Compare XSLT 2.0's built-in instruction xsl:analyze-string and its built-in function regex-group( ) for accessing captured substrings.

---

string regexp:replace(*string, string, string, string*)

This function replaces the parts of a string that match a regular expression with another string. The first argument is the string to be matched, which contains the portions to replace. The second argument is a regular expression that follows the JavaScript regular expression syntax. The fourth argument is the string to replace the matched parts of the string. The third argument is a string consisting of character flags to be used by the match. If a character is present, then that flag is true. The flags are:

g

Global replace. All occurrences of the regular expression in the string are replaced. If this character is not present, then only the first occurrence of the regular expression is replaced.

i

Case-insensitive. The regular expression is treated as case-insensitive. If this character is not present, then the regular expression is case-sensitive.

The following example replaces all instances of 2004 with 2005:

```
<xsl:value-of select="regexp:replace(
    '2004-04-14','2004','g','2005')"/>
```

The resulting string is 2005-04-14.

TIP

Compare XPath 2.0's built-in function replace( ), which includes support for referencing captured substrings (groups designated by parenthesized sub-expressions).

See also str:replace( ), later in this chapter.

boolean regexp:test(*string, string, string?*)

This function returns true if the string given as the first argument matches the regular expression given as the second argument. The second argument is a regular expression that follows the JavaScript regular expression syntax. The third argument is a string consisting of flags to be used by the test. If a character is present, then that flag is true. The flags are:

g

Global test. This has no effect on this function, but it is retained for consistency with regexp:match( ) and regexp:replace( ).

>   i

> Case insensitive. The regular expression is treated as
> case-insensitive. If this character is not present, then
> the regular expression is case-sensitive.

For example, regexp:test('Test', '[eE]') returns true.

TIP

Compare XPath 2.0's built-in function matches( ).

EXSLT—Strings

The Strings module consists of eight optional functions. The
namespace for this module is http://exslt.org/strings, and
the conventional namespace prefix is str.

Xalan-C++ claims experimental support for functions in this
module. Support information for the XSLT processors featured in this chapter is included individually with each
function.

Optional Functions—Strings Module

All of the optional Strings functions, except for str:encode-
uri( ), str:decode-uri( ), and str:concat( ), are also implemented as XSLT templates and EXSLT functions. Download
them from *http://www.exslt.org/str/*.

string str:align(*string, string, string?*)

> This function aligns a string within another string. The
> first argument gives the target string to be aligned. The
> second argument gives the padding string within which it
> is to be aligned.

> If the target string is shorter than the padding string, a
> range of characters in the padding string is replaced with
> those in the target string. Which characters are replaced
> depends on the value of the third argument, which gives

---

the type of alignment. It can be one of `left`, `right`, or `center`. If no third argument is given, or if it is not one of these values, then it defaults to left alignment.

With left alignment, the range of characters replaced by the target string begins with the first character in the padding string. With right alignment, the range of characters replaced by the target string ends with the last character in the padding string. With center alignment, the range of characters replaced by the target string is in the middle of the padding string, such that either the number of unreplaced characters on either side of the range is the same, or there is one less on the left than there is on the right.

If the target string is longer than the padding string, then it is truncated to be the same length as the padding string and returned.

For example:

```
str:align('Hello there', '-------------------------')
```

returns the string:

```
Hello there--------------
```

These processors support the `str:align()` function:

☑ 4XSLT   ☑ libxslt   ☑ Xalan-J   ☐ Saxon   ☑ EXSLT.NET

string str:concat(*node-set*)

This function takes a node-set and returns the concatenation of the string-values of the nodes in that node-set. If the node-set is empty, it returns an empty string.

TIP

Compare XPath 2.0's built-in function `string-join()`.

These processors support the `str:concat()` function:

☑ 4XSLT   ☑ libxslt   ☑ Xalan-J   ☐ Saxon   ☑ EXSLT.NET

string str:decode-uri(*string, string?*)

This function decodes a string that has been URI-encoded. The optional second argument supplies a character encoding name.

For example:

```
str:decode-uri("url-encoded%20text%20blob")
```

returns:

```
url-encoded text blob
```

These processors support the str:decode-uri( ) function:

☑ 4XSLT   ☑ libxslt   ☐ Xalan-J   ☐ Saxon   ☑ EXSLT.NET

string str:encode-uri(*string, boolean, string?*)

This function returns the first argument after URI-encoding it. If the second argument is false, then reserved URI characters are not escaped in the result. Generally, the second argument should be set to true when escaping a string that is to form a single part of a URI, and it should be set to false when escaping an entire URI. The optional third argument supplies a character encoding name.

For example:

```
str:encode-uri("url-encoded text blob",true( ))
```

returns:

```
url-encoded%20text%20blob
```

TIP

Compare XPath 2.0's built-in function escape-uri( ).

These processors support the str:encode-uri( ) function:

☑ 4XSLT   ☑ libxslt   ☐ Xalan-J   ☐ Saxon   ☑ EXSLT.NET

string str:padding(*number, string?*)

This function creates a padding string of a certain length. The first argument gives the length of the padding string to be created. The second argument gives a string to be used to create the padding. This string is repeated as many times as is necessary to create a string of the length specified by the first argument; if the string is more than a character long, it may have to be truncated to produce the required length. If no second argument is specified, it defaults to a space (" "). If the second argument is an empty string, the function returns an empty string.

For example:

```
str:padding(10,'+-+')
```

returns:

```
+-++-++-++
```

These processors support the `str:padding()` function:

☑ 4XSLT   ☑ libxslt   ☑ Xalan-J   ☐ Saxon   ☑ EXSLT.NET

node-set str:replace(*string, object, object*)

This function converts the string supplied as the first argument to a node-set by dividing the string into a series of substrings and replacing each substring with a single node. The string is divided according to a list of search strings supplied in the second argument. The third argument supplies the list of replacement nodes. Instances (in the first argument) of the *n*th search string (in the second argument) are replaced with a copy of the *n*th node in the node-set (in the third argument).

The longest substrings are replaced first. Once a replacement is made, that span of the original string is no longer eligible for subsequent replacements. An empty search string matches between every character of the original string. Unreplaced substrings are converted to text nodes.

If the second or third argument is not a node-set, it is treated as if it were a node-set containing just one text node, formed from the object's string-value.

For example:

```
str:replace($code,//replace/text,//replace/escape/)
```

will replace ' with \', " with \", etc., given an XML configuration file that looks like this:

```
<replace-config>
  <replace>
    <text>'</text>
    <escape>\'</escape>
  </replace>
  <replace>
    <text>"</text>
    <escape>\"</escape>
  </replace>
  ...
</replace-config>
```

TIP

Compare XPath 2.0's built-in function replace( ), which
uses a regular expression pattern to match the substrings
to replace (as with EXSLT's regexp:replace( ) function
described previously).

These processors support the str:replace( ) function:

☑ 4XSLT   ☐ libxslt   ☐ Xalan-J   ☐ Saxon   ☑ EXSLT.NET

node-set str:split(*string, string?*)

This function splits up a string and returns a node-set of
sibling token elements, each containing one token from
the string. The first argument is the string to be split. The
second argument is a pattern string. The string given by
the first argument is split at any occurrence of this pattern. When absent, the second argument defaults to a
space character (" ").

For example:

```
str:split('a, simple, list', ', ')
```

returns the node-set consisting of:

```
<token>a</token>
<token>simple</token>
<token>list</token>
```

TIP

Compare XPath 2.0's built-in function tokenize( ), which uses a regular expression pattern to match separator sub-strings.

These processors support the str:split( ) function:

☑ 4XSLT   ☑ libxslt   ☑ Xalan-J   ☐ Saxon   ☑ EXSLT.NET

node-set str:tokenize(*string, string?*)

This function splits up a string and returns a node-set of sibling token elements, each containing one token from the string. The first argument is the string to be tokenized. The second argument is a string consisting of a number of characters. Each character in this string is taken as a delimiting character. The string given by the first argument is split at any occurrence of any of these characters.

For example:

```
str:tokenize('2001-06-03T11:40:23', '-T:')
```

returns the node-set consisting of:

```
<token>2001</token>
<token>06</token>
<token>03</token>
<token>11</token>
<token>40</token>
<token>23</token>
```

TIP

XPath 2.0's built-in function tokenize( ), since it uses a regular expression to match separator strings, can be used to accomplish the same thing as EXSLT's str:tokenize( ).

The following processors support the str:tokenize( ) function:

☑ 4XSLT ☑ libxslt ☑ Xalan-J ☐ Saxon ☑ EXSLT.NET

XPath 1.0 Grammar

This appendix contains the entire grammar for the syntax of XPath 1.0. Refer to this section to remove any doubt about what is a syntactically valid expression.

Productions from XPath 1.0

Table 17 through Table 28 list the entire grammar of XPath 1.0, extracted from the XPath 1.0 Recommendation at *http:// www.w3.org/TR/xpath*.

Table 17. Location paths

[1]	LocationPath	RelativeLocationPath | AbsoluteLocationPath
[2]	AbsoluteLocation Path	'/' RelativeLocationPath? | AbbreviatedAbsoluteLocationPath
[3]	RelativeLocation Path	Step | RelativeLocationPath '/' Step | AbbreviatedRelativeLocationPath

Table 18. Location steps

| [4] | Step | AxisSpecifier NodeTest Predicate*
\| AbbreviatedStep |
| [5] | AxisSpecifier | AxisName '::'
\| AbbreviatedAxisSpecifier |

Table 19. Axes

[6]	AxisName	'ancestor'
		| 'ancestor-or-self'
		| 'attribute'
		| 'child'
		| 'descendant'
		| 'descendant-or-self'
		| 'following'
		| 'following-sibling'
		| 'namespace'
		| 'parent'
		| 'preceding'
		| 'preceding-sibling'
		| 'self'

Table 20. Node tests

[7]	NodeTest	NameTest
		| NodeType '(' ')'
		| 'processing-instruction'
		'(' Literal ')'

Table 21. Predicates

[8]	Predicate	'[' PredicateExpr ']'
[9]	PredicateExpr	Expr

Table 22. Abbreviations

[10]	AbbreviatedAbsoluteLocation-Path	'//' RelativeLocation-Path
[11]	AbbreviatedRelativeLocation-Path	RelativeLocation-Path '//' Step
[12]	AbbreviatedStep	'.' | '..'
[13]	AbbreviatedAxisSpecifier	'@'?

Table 23. Expressions

[14]	Expr	OrExpr
[15]	PrimaryExpr	VariableReference
		| '(' Expr ')'
		| Literal
		| Number
		| FunctionCall

Table 24. Function calls

[16]	FunctionCall	FunctionName '(' (Argument (',' Argument)*)? ')'
[17]	Argument	Expr

Table 25. Node-set expressions

[18]	UnionExpr	PathExpr | UnionExpr '|' PathExpr
[19]	PathExpr	LocationPath | FilterExpr | FilterExpr '/' RelativeLocationPath | FilterExpr '//' RelativeLocationPath
[20]	FilterExpr	PrimaryExpr | FilterExpr Predicate

Table 26. Boolean expressions

[21]	OrExpr	AndExpr | OrExpr 'or' AndExpr
[22]	AndExpr	EqualityExpr | AndExpr 'and' EqualityExpr
[23]	EqualityExpr	RelationalExpr | EqualityExpr '=' RelationalExpr | EqualityExpr '!=' RelationalExpr
[24]	RelationalExpr	AdditiveExpr | RelationalExpr '<' AdditiveExpr | RelationalExpr '>' AdditiveExpr | RelationalExpr '<=' AdditiveExpr | RelationalExpr '<=' AdditiveExpr

Table 27. Numeric expressions

[25]	AdditiveExpr	MultiplicativeExpr | AdditiveExpr '+' MultiplicativeExpr | AdditiveExpr '-' MultiplicativeExpr

Table 27. Numeric expressions (continued)

[26]	MultiplicativeExpr	UnaryExpr | MultiplicativeExpr MultiplyOperator UnaryExpr | MultiplicativeExpr 'div' UnaryExpr | MultiplicativeExpr 'mod' UnaryExpr
[27]	UnaryExpr	UnionExpr | '-' UnaryExpr

Table 28. Lexical structure of expressions

[28]	ExprToken	'(' | ')' | '[' | ']' | '.' | '..' | '@' | ',' | '::' | NameTest | NodeType | Operator | FunctionName | AxisName | Literal | Number | VariableReference
[29]	Literal	'"' [^"]* '"' | "'" [^']* "'".
[30]	Number	Digits ('.' Digits?)? | '.' Digits
[31]	Digits	[0-9]+
[32]	Operator	OperatorName | MultiplyOperator | '/' | '//' | '|' | '+' | '-' | '=' | '!=' | '<' | '<=' | '>' | '>='
[33]	OperatorName	'and' | 'or' | 'mod' | 'div'
[34]	MultiplyOperator	'*'
[35]	FunctionName	QName - NodeType
[36]	VariableReference	'$' QName
[37]	NameTest	'*' | NCName ':' '*' | QName

Table 28. Lexical structure of expressions (continued)

[38]	NodeType	'comment' | 'text' | 'processing-instruction' | 'node'
[39]	ExprWhitespace	S

Productions from Namespaces in XML

The productions listed in Table 29 are referred to directly or indirectly by the XPath grammar. They come from the XML Namespaces Recommendation at *http://www.w3.org/TR/REC-xml-names*.

Table 29. Qualified names

[4]	NCName	(Letter | '_') (NCNameChar)*
[5]	NCNameChar	NameChar - ':'[a]
[6]	QName	(Prefix ':')? LocalPart
[7]	Prefix	NCName
[8]	LocalPart	NCName

[a] This is an equivalent simplification of what's actually in the Namespaces Recommendation.

Productions from XML 1.0

The productions listed in Table 30 are referred to directly or indirectly by the XPath grammar. They come from the XML 1.0 Recommendation at *http://www.w3.org/TR/REC-xml*.

Table 30. Whitespace and name characters

[3]	S	(#x20 | #x9 | #xD | #xA)+
[4]	NameChar	Letter | Digit | '.' | '-' | '_' | ':' | CombiningChar | Extender

XSLT Pattern Grammar

Table 31 lists the entire grammar for patterns in XSLT 1.0, straight from the XSLT 1.0 Recommendation at *http://www. w3.org/TR/xslt*. The syntax for patterns is a subset of the syntax for XPath expressions.

Table 31. Patterns

[1]	Pattern	LocationPathPattern | Pattern '|' LocationPathPattern
[2]	LocationPath- Pattern	'/' RelativePathPattern? | IdKeyPattern (('/'|'//') RelativePathPattern)? | '//'? RelativePathPattern
[3]	IdKeyPattern	'id' '(' Literal ')' | 'key' '(' Literal ',' Literal ')'
[4]	RelativePath- Pattern	StepPattern | RelativePathPattern '/' StepPattern | RelativePathPattern '//' StepPattern
[5]	StepPattern	ChildOrAttributeAxisSpecifier NodeTest Predicate*
[6]	ChildOr- AttributeAxis- Specifier	AbbreviatedAxisSpecifier | ('child' | 'attribute') '::'

The AbbreviatedAxisSpecifier, NodeTest, Predicate, and Literal productions are defined in the XPath grammar. See Appendix A.

Index

We'd like to hear your suggestions for improving our indexes. Send email to
index@oreilly.com.
